ON THE STREET
WHERE YOU LIVE

Growing up in the 1950s

ON THE STREET WHERE YOU LIVE

Growing up in the 1950s

Tony Redding

To Philippa, who enjoyed a wonderful
childhood in the 1960s

This edition published in Great Britain in 2013 by DB Publishing, an imprint of JMD Media.

British Library Cataloguing in Publication Data.
A catalogue record for this book is available from the British Library.

ISBN 9781780912042

Printed and bound by Copytech (UK) Limited, Peterborough.

CONTENTS

Front cover: Empire Day – 24 May, 1954 – in the playground of Lee Manor Infants School.

Backcover: The author enjoying Open Day at Lee Green's Fire Station.

Acknowledgements

This book is a product of advancing age. As I entered my sixties I became increasingly aware of the sharp contrasts between my 1950s childhood and the complexities of life today.

I am grateful to Joy Kemp for her assistance in preparing the text and, in addition, her constant support and deep enthusiasm for the project. I also owe much to Mandy Taylor, who stood ready to help at all times.

This book is a tribute to my parents, Jack and Em Redding. Both are no longer with us. Thanks to them, I was fortunate enough to enjoy a marvellous childhood, of a type which would be very difficult to experience today.

Tony Redding,

Ash, Canterbury, Kent

March 2013

Introduction

....

We are the baby boomers!

This story of a 1950s childhood in south-east London is a nostalgic foray into a world some 60 years distant. We baby-boomers rode the shoulders of our parents and we enjoyed prosperity far beyond their dreams. Now it is our turn to reflect.

Our childhoods were free of mobile phones, computers and other gizmos. Boys wore short trousers and school caps; girls had pigtails and skipping ropes. We chewed gum, passed or failed the 11-Plus and tried to ignore the Hydrogen Bomb. Our suburban surroundings were shaped by war, the streets still pitted with bombsites, brick rubble and weeds.

I was born in 1949 and remember nothing of the very early 1950s. The first years of the new decade were much the same as the 1940s but with an important difference: Britain was no longer at war. Yet people still carried identity cards. Housewives still queued, clutching ration cards. This was a time of austerity, as victorious Britain had been bankrupted by war. Industry remained on a war footing. This time the aim was not to beat the Germans and Japanese, but simply to export enough goods to survive.

The "Credit Crunch" of 2008 saw the world enter a period of severe financial and economic crisis. Commentators talked of "the new age of austerity". Many people saw a decline in their living standards, but "austerity" is a relative term. Most people in the early 1950s had only just enough to eat, few clothes to wear, modest spending power and, apparently, very little to look forward to.

Slowly (very slowly) things got better. The 1951 Festival of Britain bravely focused on the future. Identity cards were withdrawn in 1952. A beautiful young Queen was crowned in 1953. Food rationing ended in 1954 and the *Birds Eye* fish finger arrived in 1955. Britain was on the cusp of profound change. Within just a few years there would be supermarkets, motorways, a wealth of consumer choice and the noisy cult of youth.

How can one explain to today's teenagers how kids lived in the 1950s? We played in an alien landscape, empty of *iphones*, *Facebook*, PCs, personal mobile music and the galaxy of other gadgets which now bring people together whilst, at the same time, isolating them. How can one describe the 1950s Cold War and the doctrine known as "MAD" (Mutually Assured Destruction)? It would have taken only the push of a button (in reality, the turning of keys) to vaporise our future.

The missiles sat in their silos. Nuclear bombers were armed and ready to go. A V-Bomber dropped Britain's Hydrogen Bomb on Christmas Island in October 1957. The Campaign for Nuclear Disarmament (CND) was established the following February. One of its leading lights was Canon John Collins (who, ironically, had been Chaplain to RAF Bomber Command during World War Two). Britain's nuclear capability had been of little help in 1956, when the Suez Crisis ended in humiliation.

In south-east London, wartime signs pointing to air raid shelters were still visible on walls. Shelters were of little use against the threat from new enemies, based in Moscow rather than Berlin. American schoolchildren practised ducking under their desks, but I had no such instruction. Perhaps London County Council felt this would be of no use, should the Cold War turn hot. Occasionally, an air raid siren wailed. I was never sure whether this was a Civil Defence test or merely a factory siren marking the end of the day or a shift change.

---oOo---

Shoppers of the 1950s would have laughed at the idea of paying for bottled water. Dog-walkers would have been stunned to learn that their children and grandchildren would pick up dog poo (picked up with what? There were no plastic bags!). Dog poo in the 1950s was white and disintegrated readily, presumably due to a very different doggy diet. As for their owners, relatively few people were overweight. The absence of pre-packaged ready-meals and other convenience foods showed on the waistline.

My childhood world had no quarrel with lead-based paint or, come to that, lead in petrol (added to prevent engines "pinking"). There were no car seatbelts and no airbags. Cyclists did not wear helmets. Our educational system was founded on the idea that there are always more losers than winners. This was evident in the exam results. Years later, school exams would be "dumbed down", to improve the pass rate. Kids failing to shine on a 1950s sports field received no counselling. After school, when children went out to play, they really were OUT. There were no mobiles in their pockets.

I enjoyed school. I had a nice wooden pencil box, with a sliding lid. It housed my coloured pencils and crayons. School was fun. Even the cloakrooms were great. There were long lines of safety hooks (thick doubled wire with rounded ends) and every peg had a child's name. Obviously, cloakrooms were purpose-designed by clever men for the game of chase.

---ooo---

I spent a lot of time drawing. Every now and then I received a new drawing pad from Woolworth's. The pad had a dull blue cover. Inside, the cartridge paper was creamy in colour and not especially good, but a blank sheet was always irresistible. I learnt how to make those curious paper-folds, or "wigwams", used to tell fortunes in the playground. The fancy folding turned the sheet into four triangular pockets, taking the finger and thumb of both hands. The pockets were waggled when a friend asked for a colour or number. A flap was opened up to read the message, such as "You are in love".

After school there was an occasional treat for tea – such as cheese with a miniature Hovis loaf. Delicious! At the table, when we had prunes and custard, we played that old game with the stones: "Tinker, tailor, soldier, sailor; rich man, poor man, beggar man, thief!"

South-east London in the 1950s was not entirely safe, but it certainly *felt* safe. Daily life blended the everyday and the unusual – such as when the sweep's spiky brushes suddenly emerged, with a puff of soot, from a neighbour's chimney. It was snug in my bedroom on a winter's morning. There may have been frosty whorls of ice on the inside of the window but Mum's coat, spread over my blankets, kept me cosy until it was time to get dressed for the walk to school.

I have no reason to believe my childhood was exceptional in any way. If this book triggers warm memories in the minds of readers, it serves its purpose.

---ooo---

— I —

"The Sheltered Place"

People filling my 1950s world, including Mum and Dad, had lived through the trials of the 1930s and 1940s. Their lives played out at Lee Green, in south-east London. This "London Village", just east of Lewisham, is a mile west of Eltham and a mile south of Blackheath.

Lee ("The sheltered place") was royal land from the Conquest to the early 17th-century. In 1740 there were just a dozen houses, grouped around a triangular village green. Lee later became a thriving farming and market gardening district on London's southern boundary. Its most significant building was the Manor House, built in 1722 and acquired by Sir Francis Baring, the founder of Baring Brothers.

Following Lee's enclosure in 1810, there was large-scale house-building, with the Baring estate broken up for development. Building accelerated in the 1860s with the opening of Lee Station, on the new Dartford Loop Railway. The small River Quaggy (a name derived from "quagmire") soon revealed a capacity to flood as the area became increasingly urbanised. The house-building boom was not to everyone's benefit. During the 1850s a soup kitchen was built, where the poor paid one penny for a quart of soup and a small loaf of bread.

Old and new: The Old Tiger's Head is opposite The New Tiger's Head, in the centre of Lee Green.

Lee Green became a London commuter suburb when a second railway station, Hither Green, opened in 1886. A small shopping centre grew up with grocers, general stores and other family-run shops. Lee Green's centre was dominated by two pubs, the *Old Tiger's Head* (built in 1766 and a venue for boxing matches) and the *New Tiger's Head*. My favourite building was the Fire Station, built in red brick by London County Council in 1906. Later in life I discovered that the architectural details I found so pleasing were in the "Arts and Crafts" style. The main reason why I liked the building, however, was Open Day – when we could climb all over the fire engines. My brother and I also liked to wear the firemen's heavy brass helmets – a real treat!

***Ready for anything:** Lee Green's Fire Station, with its Arts and Crafts frontage.*

Among the thousands of Victorian and Edwardian houses in Greater London destroyed by German bombs during World War Two were four homes in Taunton Road, very close to our home in Hedgley Street. The modern houses built on these bombsites during the 1950s clearly revealed where bombs had fallen. There were other casualties. The Church of the Good Shepherd, a short distance away in

Big day ... big hat: the author at the wheel of a Lee Green Fire Engine, pictured at the July 1952 Fire Brigade Fete.

Handen Road, had been gutted by fire when incendiary bombs fell on its roof in December 1940. It was not rebuilt until 1956.

Northbrook School was also destroyed by bombing. This Victorian school was built for the poor boys of the Parish, on land donated by Lord Northbrook to St Margaret's Parish Church. The school expanded, as Hedgley Street Junior and Infants School, and was renamed Northbrook School in the early 1900s. The new school, built on the bombsite, was opened by Princess Margaret in 1957. This had a typical, utilitarian post-war design, providing a light and pleasant learning environment. As an eight-year-old, I was among hundreds of children lining Manor Lane, waving flags as the Princess and her entourage swept past in large black cars.

No longer a bombsite: the 1950s-built Northbrook School, pictured just before demolition and the construction of the third school on the site. The end-terraced house at the centre of the photo is the author's former home, 48 Hedgley Street.

Lee's notable residents have included the musician Manfred Mann, the singer and songwriter Kate Bush, actress and politician Glenda Jackson, comedians Spike Milligan and Max Wall and polar explorer Sir James Clark-Ross. Karl Marx lived at Lee for a period. The vast majority of Lee's residents, however, were plain folk. My mother's parents, for example, had seen hard times. Charlie Lambert was born in Corby. His parents, Thomas and Emma, managed *The Fox*, a pub at Stonesley, near Melton Mowbray and now a private house. Charlie was unhappy at home. He took one beating too many from his father, walked out and carried on walking. He covered the 137 miles from Melton Mowbray to Lee Green, to search for work and a new life. He slept in the fields until he reached Lee and soon found steady employment as a gardener with Lewisham Council.

Charlie made Lee Green his destination as his sister, Edith, was in service locally. She found him digs with the Slade family at 17 Hedgley Street. This house was next door to Emily Sinclair, the girl who later became his wife. It was commonplace at that time to take in lodgers, to "earn a few bob". It was a tight fit at 17, as this small dwelling already housed two families.

Charlie rode with the guns of the Royal Horse Artillery during the Great War. As a Territorial he went to France in 1914, but survived to court Emily and marry her. They raised a family despite her disability. She had contracted polio as a child and walked unaided only by stooping and clasping a knee. During her young life she wore a metal leg brace and a built-up boot. The children were: Ivy (1919), my mother, Emily May (1921) and the two boys, Ted and Pete (the baby of the family, born in 1926). They lost Ted, who succumbed to TB and meningitis as a four-year-old. The household was completed by Uncle Bert, my Nan's unmarried brother. He had been gassed in the trenches and Nan had promised to look after him. He kept everyone awake at night, wheezing and coughing. Bert never went to bed, but sat up all night, dozing and struggling for breath.

Lee Green's senior generation in the 1950s: Nan is second left, second row from the front.

Illness and death were never far away. On one occasion my mother, still a young child, was taken next door to view a dead baby: "It was a girl, just two weeks old. The baby was laid out in a tiny coffin and looked just like a china doll. I was only five or six at the time."

---ooo---

The family's Victorian terraced, 15 Hedgley Street, was cramped. Mum and Ivy shared a bedroom, sparsely furnished but full. There were two single beds, a cupboard and a chest of drawers. The house had a small but pleasant garden backing onto the rear of the *Savoy* cinema and the police station.

Mum enjoyed life as a child. Northbrook School was just three minutes' walk away, at the end of the road. She was good at all sports and loved running and netball. Her close friend, Jean Harmsworth, lived next door at 13. Another friend, Alice Simpson, lived at 11. Mum's best friend, Amy Moore, lived at 28. Mum and Amy had a shared hatred of bullying teachers at Northbrook School, although there were exceptions: "One or two were nice. I remember the class in floods of tears when one of the kindly teachers died." The two pals became three with the addition of "Doll" Gunton. Her family had moved from Poplar to 32 Hedgley Street. The three girls, all born in 1921, were 13 in 1934. Mum remembers Doll's father as very strict: "Amy Moore's mother was even worse. Amy could 'play out the front', but she had to be in by the very early evening. At that time I knew who lived in every house in Hedgley Street, from 1 to 48 – which was next to the school. By 15 I had a bike and I could get around, but my world was still quite small. I no longer played in the Mews between Hedgley Street and Brightfield Road, stables at that time but later to become car repair shops. My sports were rounders and netball, but I couldn't swim. Amy Moore pushed me in on one occasion and I lost my nerve."

Close friends: Mum (Emily Lambert) with best friend Amy Moore (right). The photo was taken in Hedgley Street, before the railings were taken away for the war effort.

It might have been a spartan childhood, by today's measure, but there was always food on the table. The Lamberts had a comfortable home by 1930s standards. The food was heavy: steak and kidney pudding (cooked the old-fashioned way, in a bowl covered by muslin), toad-in-the-hole or liver and onions. Offal was popular as it was cheap. There was *Shredded Wheat* for breakfast. Nan was always busy in the morning; she took in domestic work to earn a little extra.

The surviving Lambert children had distinct personalities. Pete was the youngest and the favourite. Ivy, quiet and reserved, had a good head for academic work but suffered from "sensitive nerves". Em, my mother, was outgoing and far from bookish. The family took a week's holiday every August, staying with the grandparents at *The Fox*, near Melton Mowbray. The kids enjoyed chasing each other in the pub's garden and the occasional ride in Thomas and Emma's pony and trap. Things were not so tranquil under the surface. Charlie had not forgotten his father's fondness for belting him.

My father, Jack Redding, also had a difficult childhood. His parents lived in Deptford, south-east London. His father, Walter, had an accident, broke a leg and died in hospital when Dad was just 14. For the rest of his life he was convinced that his father should have survived and would have done, had he been able to pay for better treatment. His mother was left with four children (two boys and two girls) and no breadwinner. The problems were compounded by her addiction to "a flutter on the horses". Moonlight flits were organised, to dodge the rent man. During a low point, Dad (Jack) and his brother, Wally, went into care. They received harsh treatment and, against this background, it is easy to understand why my father married young. Both of my parents left school at 14, to contribute to the family income. Em took menial jobs and spent long hours pressing clothes at an Eltham laundry (where she earned 30 shillings in a good week). There was also shop work, including a spell at David Greig's in Woolwich.

Eventually, Mum got her first permanent job, as a coil-winder. Coil Equipment was a small factory on her doorstep, at Park Lodge – on the River Quaggy and opposite "Jimmy's", the popular *Duke of Edinburgh* pub. The girls at Coil Equipment were friendly enough but the pace was hard. Piecework ruled supreme. Mum and her workmates relaxed by going to the pictures: "Tyrone Power was my favourite. We all loved a good tear-jerker. It was a good film if we came out crying. I liked dance band music but rarely went to a dance and never went in pubs. I didn't smoke before the war but the bombing changed that."

When my parents came together, Dad was an ice-cream salesman. He pedalled a "Stop me and buy one" tricycle. With dark good looks and a reputation for cheek, he soon got a date. Later, he moved into 15 Hedgley Street to live with the Lamberts, as his mother had made life impossible. The last straw came when she pawned his only pair of shoes, then lost the money on the horses. He arrived at the Lambert home wearing plimsolls.

By the late 1930s signs of impending war were impossible to ignore. Mum said: "We didn't think about it much, but the *Blackshirts* were making a name for themselves on London streets. My Dad had been through it all before. As far as he was concerned: 'The only good German is a dead German'. And he meant it!"

Anderson Shelters appeared in back gardens: "By that time we had moved to 62 Taunton Road, just a few doors from the gate into Manor House Gardens." The family was together at 62 on the morning of Sunday 3 September, 1939. Prime Minister Neville Chamberlain made his wireless announcement that Britain, once again, was at war with Germany: "I was an innocent, having just turned 18 in March of that year. Suddenly, the whole thing hit me; I realised that life was about to change forever."

---ooo---

Jimmy Rivers was a railwayman. He was also a Territorial and when he was called up Jack Redding took his place as a Porter at Lee Station. Mum recalled: "Jack wasn't called up for a few months. We got married in late December 1939 and moved into a flat at 283 Lee High Road. It had huge rooms and the rent was just 12 shillings a week. There was a big lounge, a large bedroom, a third room and a kitchen and bathroom – which was unusual at that time. We got the flat in the November, shortly before our wedding, and spent the next few weeks decorating. Jack and Pete made a mess of wallpapering the bathroom. I put them straight."

Later, the couple ordered some *Utility* furniture, mass-produced to limited designs and basic specifications during the wartime emergency. They paid the first Hire Purchase instalment and awaited delivery, only to be told subsequently that the factory had been bombed and, that, consequently, the order would not be fulfilled. Mum gave up and bought second-hand furniture, having insisted on recovery of the HP down payment. There was no stigma attached to buying second-hand at that time. John Lewis stores, for example, had dedicated second-hand departments.

My father finally reported for service on 4 April, 1940, arriving at the *Yorkshire Grey* pub in Eltham for his medical. Mum said: "We had been married less than four months. He went away on a Monday, taking the train from Lee to London and then on to the West Country and Crownhill Fort in Plymouth."

As for the war situation, things went from bad to worse with the fall of France and the opening of the Battle of Britain. Invasion became a real possibility and Churchill made that chilling comment: "You can always take one with you." This was total war. The early casualties included the railings framing Hedgley Street's small front gardens. Teams of workmen arrived, armed with cutting torches. The railings were loaded onto the back of a lorry and driven away to be made into munitions and other war matériel. Fifteen years later, as a young child, I wondered why our front gardens were fringed with low grey stone blocks, each with a line of white blotches on top. Later, I realised that this was an echo of that day in 1940, when the men took the railings away.

This was a time when flats tended to be let by word of mouth, rather than by advertising. Em and Jack had the top flat at 283 Lee High Road. When the basement flat became available, Dad's elder brother, Wally, moved in with his wife and three children. Later that year, as the bombing became much worse, Mum moved into the then vacant ground floor flat, having decided that life at the top was becoming far too dangerous.

When Dad completed his infantry training he was posted to *The Duke of Cornwall's Light Infantry*. This regiment, first raised in 1702, became the *32nd Foot*. In the early 19th-century those regiments distinguishing themselves in battle were

Waiting for the off: The Duke of Cornwall's cross-country team gets ready outside an Eastbourne pub in 1941. The author's father, identified with a cross, was Regimental Cross-Country Champion. It is believed that the figure watching over them is Regimental Sergeant-Major "Tipper" Hicks.

honoured with the designation "Light Infantry". They marched at a brisk 140 paces a minute. Many years after the war Dad talked about the *Duke of Cornwall's* fearsome Regimental Sergeant-Major, "Tipper" Hicks. He was famed for his doom-laden order when confronting offenders: "Put him in the dungeon" (varied only by "Put him in the Glasshouse"). Hicks was born in 1905 and joined the *DCLI* at the age of 17. He became a Sergeant in 1929 and, later, an "Instructor of Musketry". Hicks was a legend in the *DCLI*. When he left the Regular Army, after the war, he became RSM of the *Cornwall Cadet Battalion*. He died in 1975 and in June 2008 his medals came up for sale.

Whilst Dad was training at Crownhill Fort Mum teamed up with another soldier's wife and visited Plymouth. Em and Jack were still newlyweds and strolled about. Mum decided to take a photograph, with Crownhill Fort in the background. There was some embarrassment when a Military Policeman strode over, seized the camera and removed the film. He administered a kindly yet stern warning about security. Mum recalled: "Jack always looked good in uniform. He was a handsome man, with jet black hair. At one point in Plymouth we struck up a conversation with an officer, who asked me what I thought of my soldier husband. I replied that he had had a good haircut but had lost too much weight.

"Back home things were happening. The sirens went almost every night and the guns on Blackheath would begin to fire. It wasn't long before I moved from the flat to Mum and Dad's at 62 Taunton Road – which had an Anderson Shelter in the garden. It felt safer together, as a family. I had been warned that the three storeys of 283 could collapse on me in a direct hit, or even a near miss. So I rejoined Mum, Dad, Ivy, Pete and Uncle Bert. We huddled inside the Anderson when the night raids began and soon made the shelter more comfortable. It was cosy in the yellow glow of the two Tilley Lamps. There was a saying during the Blitz: 'You don't hear the one that hits you'. I heard plenty; the thuds of exploding bombs set the ground vibrating."

An Anderson Shelter offered no guarantees. Three members of a family of six, sheltering in an Anderson a few streets away, were killed by a near miss. The dead were facing the entrance to the shelter. The Rescue Squad found them completely unmarked; invisible fingers of blast had reached in and squeezed the life out of them.

One afternoon a German raider dropped a stick of bombs over Lee Green. One demolished that group of houses in Taunton Road. Another destroyed Northbrook School. Fortunately, the children had been evacuated. Later in the war, Sandhurst Road School, in nearby Catford, was not so lucky. On 20 January, 1943, the school was bombed during a daylight raid and six teachers and 38 children died.

Northbrook School's ruins were a playground in the mid-1950s, with piles of bricks and dense beds of weeds. Mum told me about the bombing. Her friend, Amy Moore, had married and rented 48 Hedgley Street, next to the school. This house had been made into two flats (Mum later took over the rental and moved into the downstairs flat). When the bomb exploded, it punched a large hole into the wall adjoining the school yard. Mum was with Nan at nearby 62 Taunton Road. They emerged uninjured but black from head to toe. Soot had been forced out of the chimney by blast. The ceilings fell in and doors were blown off their hinges. Young Pete was in the toilet at the crucial moment. Mum dragged him out, ignoring his complaint that he "hadn't finished".

Changing times: looking along Hedgley Street today, with its double-parked cars and Wheelie-bins. At the end of the road is the 1950s Northbrook School, since demolished.

Bomb damage was no excuse for not turning up for work. The Coil Equipment factory was a welcoming place. Mum said: "It was a single-storey building packed with machinery and very noisy. I made good friends there. We were winding coils for depth charges. We used to sing ourselves hoarse, as there was no wireless. During the Blitz the place was hit by incendiaries and burnt out. Mr Wheeler, the factory owner, moved us into premises above the Express Dairy. Our working week was 8 am to 5.30 pm, Monday to Saturday. We had an hour for lunch and the tea came round on trolleys. It was a nice place, not too big – a real family business. Doll Gunton wanted a job and she became a coil-winder. I showed her how to do it. Mr Wheeler was kindly and gave me a corner with good light, near the window. He had two daughters. Joan was our 'Firelady' and the other daughter worked in the office. When things calmed down a bit I went to help Mr Wheeler's wife."

For a period – before the move to new premises – Mum went to work at a factory in Blackheath Village, near the railway station: "The Foreman there was awful. He even banned the girls from talking to each other. I was one of three who were the first to return to Coil Equipment. Then the others (who had been found work at Siemens in Woolwich) returned and things got back to normal. The atmosphere was wonderful – we had lots of laughs and singsongs. I took my turn, with Doll and another friend, Annie Birch, for a night's firewatching every fortnight. We had a bit of training on how to put out incendiaries. It was at that time that a German aircraft came down and flew along Lee High Road, machine-gunning all the way. The bullets sprayed the building and we threw ourselves to the floor. We then felt the pressure as bombs exploded.

"Coil Equipment had no canteen to provide meals. We took sandwiches and the factory provided the tea. We could buy snacks and sweets and chocolate were available every Saturday morning."

---ooo---

Mum often talked about friends who became victims of the Blitz, including a woman who was in a brick-built public shelter that received a direct hit. She was blown to pieces. In another terrible incident, the V1 disaster at Lewisham, another friend was vaporised: "The only thing they found was her Ration Book." This *Doodlebug* emerged from low cloud and fell on Marks and Spencer. The explosion destroyed 20 shops, damaged another 30 and killed 51 people. Over 300 shoppers were injured. The disaster happened at 9.41 am on 28 July, 1944. It was a scene of carnage. Later that year, on 25 November, a V2 rocket landed on Woolworth's at Deptford, killing 160 and injuring 200. Most of the victims were women and children.

Mum's most powerful wartime memory came from the Blitz: "I went to the pictures with Doll. When we came out of the *Savoy* the sky was bright red – London was on fire. Doll's face was red, reflecting the glow. We ran towards the back of the fish and chip shop and took shelter under a cart as shrapnel rained down. Eventually, it was safe enough to run for home. The pavements were covered in shrapnel."

There was also the night my Dad, home on leave, helped Charlie ("Pop") and a neighbour, Bill Fisher, to put out an incendiary. They were shovelling earth over it when it blew up. Around one in 10 incendiaries carried an explosive charge, to deter firefighters. The blast caught Bill Fisher and peppered his face and body with hundreds of shrapnel fragments. They carried him inside, laid him on the kitchen table and began to bathe his wounds. For years afterwards, Bill went to hospital regularly, to have metal removed.

---ooo---

In the 1950s our small garden at 48 Hedgley Street still had its Anderson Shelter (which wouldn't have been much use against Russian H-bombs). It was filled with junk and had a few inches of smelly water in the bottom. It had lost its protective coating of soil and the steel sheeting was exposed. These shelters were named after Sir John Anderson, who was put in charge of Britain's Air Raid Precautions before the Blitz. Over two million homes had Anderson Shelters. They were supplied free to the poor but those earning over £5 a week had to buy one for £7. The Anderson was formed of curved steel plates, recessed 4ft into the ground. The 6ft 6in by 4ft 6in shelter could accommodate six at a squeeze.

When the war ended, Coil Equipment's Mr Wheeler wanted to celebrate by treating his girls to a dinner. Instead, Mum suggested it would be better to organise a group photograph: "It was something we could keep. Only a few of our girls were missing that day. Mr Ralph, a photographer based in Taunton Road, took an impressive photo of Coil Equipment's workforce."

Victory photo: the girls of Coil Equipment Ltd. Mum is fourth from right, in the front row. Her close friend, Annie Birch, is on her left.

---ooo---

It is difficult to describe the anarchic beauty of bombsites. The remains of Northbrook School looked like a set for a war film. It was full of hiding places for adventurous kids. Pedestrians had worn a diagonal short-cut across the bombsite, cutting the corner of Taunton Road and Hedgley Street.

During the 1950s one of my Aunts lived in a "prefab", a prefabricated home built immediately after the war to help ease the housing shortage. Over 100,000 London homes had been destroyed and a million more damaged. Prefabs were seen as a temporary solution, to be occupied for up to 10 years – giving enough time for the major slum clearances to make progress. Yet, some prefabs were still occupied over 50 years later. Those still living in them were enthusiasts, fiercely loyal and refusing all alternatives. Immediately after the war, prefabs, with bathrooms and "all mod cons" were heaven-sent to those brought up in pre-war slum housing. Over 150,000 prefabs were built.

In 2005 I visited Lee Green and found just one surviving railing stone in Hedgley Street. It still bore the scars of the day the railings were removed, 65 years earlier. This was a reminder of a time before satellite dishes, wheelie bins and wall-to-wall cars. A short stroll down Hedgley Street is the *Duke of Edinburgh*, now offering live Irish music rather than sing-songs around the piano. The small river running between back gardens and through the park is defended today by "QWAG", the Quaggy Waterways Action Group, dedicated to restoring this urban stream for the benefit of "wildlife, education, amenity and beauty..."

Today, people can take as many photos as they like at Plymouth's Crownhill Fort. This Victorian fortress, rescued by The Landmark Trust, is the sole surviving Victorian fort with an unchanged layout. Crownhill Fort is now a tourist attraction and a venue for corporate and private entertaining. A daily gun fires on the parade ground; Cappuccino and Danish pastries are available in the *Retreat Café*. There are no Military Police around.

---ooo---

— 2 —

Changing Times, Rising Expectations

....

Life in early 1950s Britain had changed little. There was no popular teenage culture. Few people questioned authority. There were plenty of uniforms around, with compulsory military service for young men. The Cold War and its hot sideshow, the Korean conflict, continued the lengthy confrontation between democracies and dictatorships. It was more of the same, with rationing and austerity the order of the day in a country close to bankruptcy.

Yet, this was a time when men and women took responsibility for themselves. They made up their own minds, as the "Nanny State" was still in its cradle. They could smoke themselves to death if they wished. Health and safety were matters largely confined to the workplace. Cars had no seat belts, airbags or child seats. There were no "best before" dates on food. Meat, cheese and milk were checked with the eyes and nose. There was only modest consumer choice. There were no fridges and milk bottles were stood in pails of water during the Summer. Home entertainment amounted to the wireless, reading and gardening. Going out meant going to the pictures or to the pub. There was little disposable income but few people borrowed money. The only credit available to most was HP. Heavy industry dominated the economy and the smog problem was aggravated by millions of domestic coal fires.

Parents and teachers assumed schoolchildren would not have sex before the age of 16. Indeed, it was assumed that they wouldn't have sex before marriage. Naughty and rude children were thrashed or thumped (given a "thick ear"). This offered clear guidance on what was right or wrong. As for adults, men and women in their late sixties were regarded as old. Anyone reaching 80 was ancient and people in their nineties were rare. Couples got engaged and married; they did not "live in sin" and few children were born out of wedlock. Only five per cent of parents were unmarried. Their children were known (by whispering neighbours) as "bastards" and were often given up for adoption out of a sense of shame. There was also shame in divorce, regardless of the division of fault. There was no contraceptive pill and no morning after pill.

This thumbnail of the 1950s makes it sound bloody miserable, but that was not the case! People enjoyed life and communities were well connected. It was safe for kids to play outside and mothers walked their children to school. Housewives shopped daily and often stopped to chat on street corners. People knew their neighbours and many knew virtually every family living in their road or street. There was very little in the way of state support, but there was always plenty of help available from friends and extended families living close to each other.

There was less social and community mobility in the 1950s. People tended to live in the same area for most of their lives. They were also accustomed to helping each other. Few people went into "care" – their families looked after them until they were whisked away by stroke, heart attack or pneumonia. Generally, there was much less pressure on resources, as the total population was still under 50 million in the early 1950s.

Everything changed in the five years to 1960. Suddenly, there were teenagers, pop music, serious challenges to authority, Britain's first nuclear power station and the silicon chip (invented in 1958). Harold MacMillan's "winds of change" speech referred to the end of Empire and the desire for independence. Yet his phrase also described what was happening within British society. Television took a firm hold, the BBC lost its monopoly, race riots broke out in Notting Hill, the Soviet Union's *Sputnik* orbited the Earth and Britain's first motorway opened. We were just a couple of years away from the *Telstar* communications satellite and *Beatlemania* and only 10 years from the Moon landing and *Concorde's* maiden flight.

People came to regard a steady rise in living standards as theirs by right. There was room for expectations: only one household in 10 had a telephone and a car was still out of reach for many working men. The average weekly wage was £7.28 in 1950, but almost doubled to £14.10 by 1960. Harold MacMillan told my parents: "You've never had it so good!"

---ooo---

How did the 1950s feel? Well, it felt GOOD. It was very safe. People living in Lee Green did not leave their keys in the door but, equally, they did not barricade themselves in with multiple locks, chains and burglar alarms. Commercial premises had yet to be draped with reefs of razor wire. Kids under 10 walked to school unescorted and people went out on Saturday night without fear of being mugged or blinded by a broken bottle. There were no swarms of drunken youths, behaving aggressively and vomiting over themselves. The worst case might be a lone drunk, singing *Show me the way to go home.*

Ironically, this safe and cosy world was just an illusion. At the age of six or seven, I did not appreciate that, only a few years before, some 60 million people had died in an appalling world war filled with barbarism and depravity. It is difficult to reconcile this with the world of *Janet and John* reading books and *Watch with Mother*. The evidence of bombing stood just a few feet from our front gate: the wreckage of Northbrook School. I had no understanding of the context of our lives. I had no idea that my parents – like all others – were still adjusting. Most 1950s parents, all too well aware of the fragility of life and "civilisation", worked extremely hard to create a safe, secure environment for their children.

Dear Child, here is a candle newly lit,
You are so small you cannot understand,
But we who watch will fearless tend the light,
Knowing God holds you in His loving hand.

A safe and cosy world: the card issued by the Church of the Good Shepherd, Lee, following Baptism.

Slowly, however, reality encroached. By the late 1950s I was aware that the Cold War might suddenly become hot (hotter, in fact, than the surface of the Sun). People on television talked about the "Four Minute Warning" (just enough time to tell everyone that they were about to die). Weapons testing was big news, with the Americans and Russians locked into a competition to detonate the largest possible hydrogen bomb. There was even a "neutron bomb". Apparently, this burst with a relatively modest explosion but produced a catastrophic wave of radiation, killing everything in a city yet leaving the buildings standing.

Kids bedrooms in the 1950s were not playrooms. They were for sleeping only. I huddled in my bed, in the small bedroom at the back of 48 Hedgley Street, and tried to sleep. I thought about those Russian rockets, all aimed at me! Electric flashes from the nearby railway could be the real thing: the last thing I would ever see. With the morning the safe and secure world returned. I ate my porridge or cornflakes and toast, then walked to school with my leather satchel, cap and blazer. What could possibly go wrong?

---ooo---

My grandparents lived by a simple maxim: "If we can't afford it, we can't have it". It was a case of forget it or save... very slowly. My parents had more flexibility, with the availability of *Easy Terms*, or *HP*. Yet the market itself was inflexible. "Resale Price Maintenance" allowed for little in the way of price competition (and there were no supermarkets offering huge discounts). The price was the price: take it or leave it!

Televisions and other electrical goods were expensive. A 17 inch television in 1958 cost 67 guineas, but could be rented for 11 shillings a week. Most people rented as the agreement included free maintenance. Televisions in the 1950s often went wrong. Around one in seven families owned a car in 1950. This had more than doubled, to one in three, by 1959 – reflecting a major increase in spending power. Nevertheless, it was always difficult to find the money for a rapidly expanding range of labour-saving household gadgets, such as the "twin tub" washing machine. A washing machine was four to five times more expensive, in relative terms.

Some things were cheaper, notably beer, cigarettes and property. House prices in the 1950s were over four times cheaper. Even so, most people rented and it was commonplace for two families to share a small terraced home. The average house price in 1957 was £2,120 – a figure beyond most pockets. Some years earlier, Mum and Dad had the chance to buy 48 Hedgley Street for £500 but felt it beyond their means. In 1973, I bought my first house: a small mid-terraced property in a Kent coastal town. It cost £6,500. As for 48 Hedgley Street, this modest end of terrace sold for £275,000 in October 2005. The current value, at the time of writing, is put at around £344,000.

Once a bargain: the author's parents decided against buying 48 Hedgley Street for £500! Next door is the 1950s Northbrook School, now replaced by a new and larger school. The modern car is exactly where Ford Popular GUN 481 stood over 50 years earlier.

Standard equipment in the 1950s home included a vacuum cleaner, wireless and cooker. Only one-third of households acquired a washing machine during the 1950s (we didn't). Only 15 per cent of homes had a fridge in 1957 (we didn't). Clothes were washed and dried by hand, using a copper boiler, a mangle and "horses", to lay out the clothes to dry in front of the fire on rainy days. Fitted carpets were rare. Linoleum was the more usual floor covering, enhanced by a few rugs. Our "scullery" was both kitchen and laundry. We had a cold water tap over a large stone sink and a wall-mounted *Geyser* provided a limited supply of hot water. Most 1950s homes lacked bathrooms. Our toilet was in the back garden (a brick outhouse, attached to an outer wall of the scullery). The tin baths (one long and one oval) hung on nails in the wall, outside the door to the toilet.

We had no central heating. There was a coal fire in the rear sitting room and a gas fire in the front room. Paraffin heaters warmed bedrooms on cold winter nights. I loved our cylinder paraffin heater, with its gentle popping noise, pleasant smell (probably due to noxious fumes) and the light pattern it projected onto the ceiling. It had the personality of an old, comforting friend.

Life at our home was regulated by Nan's wise sayings: "All that glitters is not gold"; "Don't make a mountain out of a molehill"; "Children should be seen and not heard"; and, of course, "If you can't say something nice about someone, say nothing".

During the first half of the 1950s women were expected to be content as mothers and homemakers, rather than wage-earners. This reflected the adjustment at the end of the war, when men demobbed from the forces returned to jobs performed by women whilst they were away. Increasingly, however, women sought to contribute to the family income. In most cases this was not to buy luxuries but, rather, to pay for the children's clothes or Christmas presents.

Mum worked Saturdays in Oxenburghs, the soft furnishings store in Lewisham. She was also a childminder. There were no inspections, CRB checks and other bureaucracy – just a private, informal arrangement with the parents. There was a need for more childminders as increasing numbers of women began working full-time. The Playgroup movement was not launched until 1960 and the number of nursery places available had declined sharply after the war (when the Central Government grant for nurseries was halved). The number of casual childminders tripled in the 1950s and 1960s.

Throughout the 1950s we never went short. Bills were paid (often before they were due) and our larder was well stocked. Yet 1950s life had a tough edge: until mid-decade over 70 per cent of the workforce was engaged in manual labour. The five-day week was an innovation, rather than a standard. My father did a four and a half day week for a very low wage, but doubled his money working Friday and Saturday nightshifts. In the white collar work environment, attitudes were formal. It was "Mr Jones", not "David" or "John". Professional people – doctors, teachers, solicitors, bank managers and the like – had real status.

---ooo---

These adult matters were of little interest to me, although I was, perhaps, an unusually acute observer for my age. I had an eye for the detail of life. The horse and cart was still a common sight on the street. The Rag and Bone Man made his rounds, calling "Any old iron?" His words were castrated and came out as a dull, rather high-pitched yelp. He took away the sort of rubbish people now buy at car boot sales and make cheap television programmes about.

In our small back garden I was content, playing with a toy of its time – a red plastic rocket. Its nosecone contained a deadly warhead of caps. When indoors I spent a lot of time reading. One of my favourites was a large hardback volume, *I flew with Braddock* (George Bourne), describing the adventures of an RAF bomber crew during the war. These stories were originally published in the *Rover* comic.

I went to the nearby park to play. I was too old for chase games, but groups of younger children were playing "it" on the grass. They were "dibbing" in a circle to the chant: "Ib, dib, dog shit, you are it!" I played football with my friends; coats and jumpers formed the goals. When not playing football, I went on nature hunts – exploring for butterflies, moths and beetles. There was an astonishing variety of exotic caterpillars and moths in that suburban park during the 1950s (before these creatures were rendered extinct by agrochemical sprays). My favourites were *Tiger Moths, Hawk Moths* and their caterpillars.

The popular crazes included hula hoops and yo-yos. I loved plasticine, although it gave my hands a rather disgusting smell after a while. I had no ipod or mobile phone, but I did have two tin cans connected by string. With the string pulled tight, the reception was often better than from my 21st-century mobile.

---ooo---

It is time to describe our home, 48 Hedgley Street, in more detail. It was an end terrace next to Northbrook School. It had two living rooms, a scullery and three bedrooms. The house was of yellow brick, with a slate roof. There was a very small front garden, perhaps 2 m wide, consisting of a small flower bed under the lower bay window and a narrow path, behind a low brick wall. To the rear was a small garden, with an outside toilet, a small shed with a tar-felt roof and a creosoted fence on the short perimeter bordering the school.

The front room contained a red three-piece suite of generous proportions and a rather ugly, glass-fronted "bureau". In its display wings were examples of the green and pinkish-brown glassware given to my parents as wedding presents in December 1939. The room was heated by a gas fire. In the window bay was a substantial *Pedigree* pram. It had once housed me, then my brother and, finally, my younger sister, Janet. The front window bay was the only parking space available for this comfortable but ungainly carriage. On the gas fire side of the bay was the dark brown cabinet of our 12 inch television set. On the wall, over the fireplace, was a heavy mirror, hanging by a chain from the "picture rail". The central ceiling light sported a large, tasselled shade.

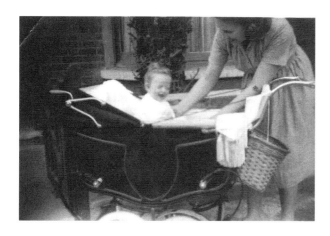

Very comfortable: the author pictured in his pram, later occupied by a brother and a sister.

The rear living room had a coal fire and built-in cupboards to one side of the chimney-breast. This room had a *Utility* table and chairs and two more comfortable chairs by the fire. There was also a small sideboard with a wireless. A portable wind-up gramophone of 1930s or 1940s vintage sat on a small table in one corner. There was a window looking out at the "backyard", providing a view of the two tin baths hanging on the wall, together with the rather ramshackle wartime Anderson Shelter.

There was a coal bucket by the hearth and a spark-guard covered the fire opening. The fire was lit and drawn using newspaper wrapped over the spark-guard. This was not without its dangers. The paper would begin to smoulder if left in place for too long. There was also the danger of a chimney fire, if the updraught was maintained for any length of time.

Along the passageway leading to the scullery was a large, walk-in cupboard which contained the electricity meter, fuse wire, some basic tools and the means to repair sash windows. It also contained our cylinder vacuum cleaner (always known as "The Hoover"), brooms and a mop and bucket. The cupboard always smelt faintly of *Dettol*.

The final room downstairs, the scullery, was both kitchen and washroom. There was a step down into this room. I made Mum panic when, at the age of four, I fell down the step and put my bottom front teeth through my lip. I don't remember the accident, but still sport a small white scar.

The scullery was well-appointed, with the equipment including a cream-coloured gas cooker with an eye-level grill in a hood-like structure. There was a large glazed sink under the window, with the *Geyser* providing hot water mounted on the wall close by. The curtain under the sink hid a bucket, scrubbing brush and a box of dusters and cleaning materials. A shelf was loaded with Ajax, a large block of yellow coal tar soap, a packet of washing soda in a blue box and a sink plunger.

Nearby was a 1950s-style kitchen cabinet in blue and cream, with a pull-down flap. Inside its cupboards were plates, cups and mixing bowls.

Opposite the window was the "copper", where the washing was done, with its bleached copper stick propped up nearby. When my brother was naughty, Mum chased him with the copper stick, but the threat was never carried out. There was also the mangle, to squeeze out water from the washing. On the ceiling were hooks for a large drying frame, but this had been removed. In its place were two "clothes horses" – wooden frames with fabric ties. They were placed in front of the rear living room fire when the winter weather was too bad to use the garden line.

Having a bath in the scullery was a real performance, a once-a-week event due to the sheer effort involved. The long tin bath was lifted in from the backyard. Slowly, it was filled to the half-way mark by bucket after bucket of hot water. It took forever to achieve enough depth for a bath. I was always first and managed to leave the next in line a thin film of white soap scum on the surface.

A friend of mine also has memories of bath night. On one occasion he farted and had an accident. The evidence soon bobbed to the surface. His horrified mother scooped up the offending turd and snapped "Say nothing!" as the next child arrived for a bath. She could not face emptying the bath and repeating the process. Bucketing out was a major job and it was always tempting to try to remove the heavy bath with too much water still inside. It would then begin to slop dangerously as the bath was manoeuvred out of the back door.

Moving to the first floor, our stairs were carpeted and finished with gleaming brass stair-rods. The first flight of stairs ended in a small area fronting the small bedroom to the rear, occupied by the children. The upper hallway, reached by a few more stairs, led to the larger rear bedroom, occupied by Nan and Ivy (until she died), with the front bedroom for Mum and Dad. When in my small bedroom I would open the sash window and study the sky and the back gardens of the next road as I picked off the peeling green paint of the timber window ledge.

---ooo---

Occasionally, during the school holidays, I would be dragged along on a shopping trip. Lee Green's small parade of shops was just five minutes away. Mum tied on her headscarf, folded into a triangle and secured under the chin. This made a change from her turban, tied at the forehead – a style for working around the home or buffing the front doorstep with red *Cardinal* polish.

I was five years old when food rationing ended in July 1954. I noticed little change. People still queued obediently outside the shops. Lee Green had a bakers, fishmonger, greengrocer and butchers. Everyone paid in cash; there were no credit cards in purses or wallets. Food was seasonal and there were few imported fruits and vegetables. Chicken was expensive as battery production was still some years away. Everyone was served at the counter – no-one served themselves. In the newsagents a wide range of cigarettes was on display, all free of health warnings. A 1954 report concluded that smoking causes cancer yet this warning went unheeded. Almost everyone smoked and young people were encouraged by clever advertising. Lack of money was no barrier to entry, as most shops were willing to sell one or two cigarettes and a couple of matches. The sale of "bike shed smoking kits" continued well into the 1960s. As a hard-up art student, during the mid-1960s, I occasionally went to the corner shop to buy a single cigarette. I would smoke half and put it out, saving the rest for later.

Everything was priced in pre-decimal "old money": pounds, shillings and pence (240 pence to the pound). Twelve pence made a shilling and 20 shillings made a pound. Expensive items were priced in guineas (21 shillings). There were farthings (a quarter of an old penny), together with larger ha'pennies. There was also the dodecagonal (12-sided) threepence (three old pennies), an attractive and chunky, greenish nickel-brass coin. The word was pronounced "thruppence"; some knew the coin as a "thruppenny bit". The silver-coloured sixpence (a "tanner") was worth 2.5p; the shilling (a "bob") was worth 5p and a florin ("two bob") 10p. The best coin was the hefty half-crown, worth 12.5p. Paper money included the ten shilling note ("ten bob"), worth 50p, and the £1 note. Spending power, of course, was much greater than that of the equivalents today.

Shopping was a daily social ritual. Housewives went out to shop and gossip, but not necessarily in that order. I remember being stuck as Mum chatted with one of her friends about a woman who was a Roman Catholic and could not divorce her violent husband. I found it very dull and failed to appreciate why it took half an hour to tell the story.

This was a world without fast food, other than fish and chips. *McDonalds* and *Kentucky Fried Chicken* belonged to the future. Housewives bought fresh food for the next day or two and there was very little waste. There was nothing unusual in the shopping bag. "Afters", for example, might be stewed apple and custard, or sliced banana and custard. We had tinned peaches or pineapple chunks with condensed milk on Sundays. On Mondays, there might be bread and dripping as a snack, with rich brown jelly from the Sunday beef joint. I always felt this was Dad's by right, but occasionally enjoyed a slice. Exotic items came our way on rare occasions. Dad arrived home from one night shift with a bag of lychees. A ganger had a brother who was a docker. I had never seen anything so unlikely and had no idea how to eat it. I thought its perfumed taste wonderful, although Mum said it was like eating fruity *eau de cologne*.

---oOo---

Some people say there was nothing good about the 1950s. Most people were hard up, poorly educated and did a lot more physical work. Typically, men lived only a few years after retiring at 65. Boys played with toy guns and were forever pretending to die in battle. Everyone, young or old, had to conform. Did we have it so good? The answer will depend on what you, the reader, regards as important in life.

Respectability was all-important in the 1950s. Teddy Boys were seen as heralds of a more self-centred, antisocial future. Generally, authority still held sway. The Bobby on the beat, teachers, parents, park-keepers, bus conductors and vicars maintained the status quo.

Today, of course, we inhabit another planet. Is it pleasant living in a society without taboos? Subjects regarded as grossly obscene in the 1950s are now common fare on television and in other media. In just 50 years we have travelled to an extreme horizon, a place where the only sin is to be shocked.

---oOo---

The 1960s social revolution soon crushed the 1940s and 1950s lifestyle. By the mid-1960s over half the British workforce was employed in service industries, rather than manufacturing. By 1961, 75 per cent of families had TV and *Coronation Street* had just begun. Britain's population rose by three million in just 10 years.

The 1970s was shaped by technology. The computer mouse was patented in 1970, the year the first Jumbo Jets entered service. Microsoft was established in 1975. Domestic microwaves had just been launched and the first video game console was on sale. The Sony *Walkman* arrived. This was the decade of "rights". The Equal Pay Act took effect in 1970 and the Commission for Racial Equality began operating in 1977.

The population of Britain had grown to over 56 million by 1981. The average weekly wage for men was £127.70, but only £75.70 for women (the Equal Pay Act lacked punch). The 1980s saw the launch of Breakfast TV, the rise of out-of-town supermarkets, the first version of Microsoft *Windows*, brick-sized mobile telephones and CDs. Cinema ticket sales slumped, from over 340 million to less than 55 million, in the 20 years to 1984.

By the early 1990s over half of all women were in work. Nearly 70 per cent of all people in employment worked in the service industries. In 1950 Britain had 690,000 coal miners. In 1994, there were just 17,000, following changes in the fuel mix, the flood tide of cheap coal imports and the unions' disastrous confrontation with Margaret Thatcher.

By 1991 25 per cent of parents were unmarried and around one-third of marriages ended in divorce. By way of compensation, virtually every home had a washing machine. The population reached 58 million, with 10 per cent non-white or of mixed-race. The World Wide Web was launched in 1991 and there were 130 million web users in the world by 1998.

This tidal wave of change continued during the first decade of the new Millennium. The process was marked by growing social dependence, "dumbing down" and the build-up of unsustainable levels of debt. Britain's population approached 61 million, with two thirds of population growth relating to immigration. Between 1948 and 1970 around half a million people left the West Indies to live in Britain.

By the middle of the first decade of a new century, 12 per cent of the population was 85 or over. By 2007 Britain had more pensioners than teenagers. Over 40 per cent of mothers were unmarried and around 25 per cent of children lived in one parent families. Half of lone parents were not in work. In 2005 (three years before the 2008 financial and economic crash), some 850,000 people were claiming "Jobseeker's Allowance". This had increased to over one million by 2008. Yet, around 70 per cent of UK households now had a DVD player, over 50 per cent had Internet access and the number of mobile telephones in use exceeded the UK population. The new communication tools proved useful when organising the Summer riots of 2011.

My generation came to regard debt as part of normal life. Our children know no other way. By 2004, Britain had more credit cards than people. The old phrase "Live now, pay later" came home to roost in 2008, when everyone (except those arch rogues, the bankers) began to pay.

With hindsight it is always easy to recognise mistakes and blind alleys. Tower blocks were *not* a solution to urban housing needs. Unfettered immigration and those criminal political failures allowing mass illegal immigration have increased social and economic pressures. There has been a disastrous loss of community. In its place we have remote human interaction: mobiles, emails, texts, tweets and whatever fad happens to be next. Around one-third of all households consist of people who live alone. The loss of social cohesion over the past 50 years has been dramatic, traumatic and catastrophic.

Social attitudes and manners have changed beyond recognition, as Church, State, institutions, police and the "ruling class" lost their grip. Too much freedom and too much choice are curses rather than blessings. Today, the ultimate "right" is to be free to express individuality; too bad if that expression is at the expense of society. When Margaret Thatcher declared "There is no such thing as society", she was delivering an accurate summary of the state of Britain. Her successors have spoken of the "broken society", but no-one knows how to fix it... if it still exists to fix.

The Age of Simplicity has been swallowed whole by the Age of Complexity. The low-cost amateur childminder is out of favour, due to over-regulation and a host of other factors. As a result, childcare is beyond the means of many. In 2012 the Daycare Trust published a survey revealing that some parents now spend more on childcare than on their mortgages. The most expensive nursery was in London and charged £24,000 annually for a full-time place. The Trust concluded that parents in the south-east of the country, with two children in childcare, are likely to spend around the same or more for childcare than for their mortgage.

---ooo---

This journey of nearly six decades has taken the everyday experience of living in Britain a long way from the stable social environment of the 1950s. As late as 1959, my Dad's mother lived in a first floor flat in a terraced house in Greenwich. It had no electricity; she had gas lighting and her wireless was powered by acid-filled accumulator batteries. Now most people (at least those fortunate enough to still have a job) have fitted carpets, fridges, freezers, washing machines, fitted kitchens, widescreen TVs, DVD players, computers, mobiles, two or more cars and the expectation of at least two holidays a year. Yet they also eat 21st-century rubbish and live life at a fast pace, to paper over the cracks caused by lack of community. There is no respect and little sense of belonging. In 1957 the police recorded just over half a million offences. In 1997, the figure was 4.5 million. In 40 years violent crimes against the person increased from below 11,000 to 250,000.

---ooo---

- 3 -

"Infants and Juniors"

In 1954 I was about to start school. As the great day neared, I was playing at the front garden gate when a girl of about 11 stopped to chat. She asked me what school I would be going to. This harmless question threw me into confusion. I had not appreciated that schools had names and that, secondly, there was more than one school to choose from. I turned, ran inside and repeated the question to Mum.

The answer was Lee Manor Infants and Junior School, a gentle harbour for small children. The Infants' classrooms had small desks and tiny chairs and I was shown to mine. At the end of the day we had to up-end our chairs and slide them onto the desks, so allowing the cleaners an unobstructed sweep. Only a few years before, during World War Two, this school had been a base for the Auxiliary Fire Service. The school building was of red-orange brick and the accommodation was single-storey. Inside, the wood block floors were highly polished, with no litter around. Everything was spic and span and carried a pleasant odour of school, *Lifebuoy* soap and beeswax. There were beanbags everywhere. Beanbags were very important in 1950s Infants' schools. There is nothing menacing about a beanbag – it could be thrown around without fear of hurting anyone. Beanbags came in all shapes and sizes, including those just right for a small child's grip.

A recent photo of Lee Manor School: its orange brickwork is now part-rendered.

Our class teacher, Miss White, was an elderly, kindly soul who would have been surprised at anything other than good behaviour. There was also Miss Williams, a tall blonde lady of late middle age and another gentle soul. For these women (and many thousands like them) teaching was more than a job. It was a way of life that had demanded stern choices. Women teachers who married had to leave the profession. Yet, our spinster teachers all had families; we were their kids and, perhaps for that reason, our relationship was subtly different to that found in today's classroom. All Infants' teachers were addressed as "Miss".

Miss Williams' class in the mid-1950s: the author, looking rather lost, is at the far right, top row. Visible is that highly polished pine block floor.

Young children were walked to school by their mothers, who also collected them in the afternoon. Many Mums pushed babies and infants in large prams and pushchairs. The area around the school gates was always crowded and noisy. Traffic congestion was not the issue: the school run was still many years away. The problem resulted when women stopped to chat, mindless of the traffic jam caused by their gigantic prams.

The school day began with the Register and Assembly. There was hymn singing and prayers. With lessons finally under way, we opened our *Janet and John* reading books. We practiced multiplication tables, chanting together in that harmonious sing-song rhythm. There were toys to play with later. The long pole propped up in the corner of our classroom was not for beating children, but used to hook open the high windows in warm weather. There was a large blackboard and plenty of chalk at the ready. All activities were undertaken under the benevolent gaze of Miss White.

One annual highlight at Lee Manor Infants' School was "Empire Day". I was one of its last celebrants. We waved our Union Flags as we marched around the playground, watched by doting parents. They then took us home, as we were given the afternoon off. Empire Day was introduced to remind children that they were fortunate indeed to be part of the British Empire. The idea had originated in Canada during the late 1890s. Queen Victoria died in January 1901 and the first Empire Day was celebrated on 24 May the following year (the old Queen's birthday). Later, it became an annual event, at home and abroad.

A few years on, now in Junior School, I walked to and from school unescorted. I carried a brown leather satchel, secured by two buckles. Happily, I lived close enough to return for lunch. I felt privileged to avoid the Dinner Ladies' boiled vegetables and semolina.

Ready for school: the author (left) with brother Colin. Sister Janet is still some way from the start of her school career.

On at least one occasion I had a lift to school. Dad sat behind the wheel of our Ford *Popular*. This was probably in September 1956, just after the Summer holidays. Dad dropped me at the school gate and warned that the car would have to be taken off the road if petrol rationing got any worse. Egypt's President Nasser had seized the Suez Canal that July. Dad must have had time off as the working week was reduced during the Suez emergency.

Junior School had a different atmosphere and, in many ways, was more fun. Sometimes I was reluctant to get out of bed on a winter's morning, but I always enjoyed school. In the 1950s truancy was rare. Certainly, the thought of skipping school never crossed my mind. I found the lessons interesting but was never much good at games – although I loved playing football. In the Summer, cricket nets almost filled the rather scruffy small field in the school grounds. I was never interested in cricket and still, to this day, have no knowledge of the rules of the game.

We Juniors were blessed with good teachers. Our class teacher, Mr Leale, was in his early fifties. He was ruddy-faced, balding, wore spectacles and sported an olive/brown tweed jacket with elbow patches. Between the wars, he had served in the Royal Air Force as ground crew for biplane fighter squadrons. This fine man had a very warm personality but stood no nonsense. Unlike my mother – who had feared her teachers at Northbrook School a generation before – I felt only trust in my relationship with Lee Manor's teachers. This relationship was extremely stable; it was rare for a teacher to shout at a pupil.

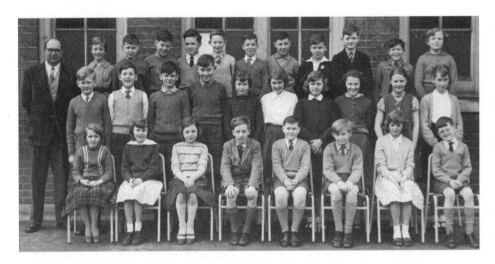

Mr Leale's class of the late 1950s. The author is in the front row (third from right). After over 50 years, the author can name 20 of his 28 classmates.

Mr Herbert, the Headmaster, was a quiet, imposing man who kept himself aloof, in keeping with his station. He was in late middle age and quite handsome, with regular features and silver-grey hair. Mr Herbert was perfectly prepared to cane boys, but only those who richly deserved it (including, on repeated occasions, my brother).

Lee Manor was a mixed establishment. At that time I knew girls were "different" (although my understanding of the differences was rudimentary). I had various "girlfriends", including Jeanette Edmonds and Helen Govan. It was all very innocent, with only an occasional faltering kiss.

Sex education was unheard of at Lee Manor School. Indeed, I left school at 16, in 1965, without having experienced a single sex education lesson (despite having attended three grammar schools in four years, due to house moves). In biology, however, some attention had been paid to the reproductive rites of single-celled organisms and the life-cycle of the frog. Some boys fumbled with girls in the playground, their activities hidden from view by coats obligingly held by the next girl to take her turn. I had no interest here. I could see nothing alluring about this, having come across colourful cross-sections of human genitalia in Mum's *Home Doctor* book. It seemed to me that God's handiwork lacked artistic finesse. The *Home Doctor* double-page spread put me off further investigation for a year or two. When, at the age of 11, a friend told me what men and women did together, I refused to believe him. When he insisted it was true, I found the whole idea disgusting. I went home, waited for Mum to go out and consulted the *Home Doctor*, to see how things might fit together.

Somewhat later, when sharing a few kisses and some groping in a park shelter with an unusually bold girl, I found something peculiar happening to me. In fact, it was so peculiar that it was impossible to go straight home. I walked round the block, with my red plastic football clutched in a strategic place. Things eventually returned to normal and I made for home. I had no idea, at that time, that what goes up also goes down!

---ooo---

Corporal punishment flourished at Lee Manor, despite its happy and protective atmosphere. I was never caned, but my brother, Colin, was said to have been the most-caned boy in school. The cane was reserved for boys, although girls may have been chastised occasionally, with strokes from a ruler on the palm of the hand. Lee Manor kept a *School Punishment Book*, a handsome, cloth-bound volume with meticulous entries. Fifty years later, having discovered this relic in the two cardboard boxes which now constitute the school's 1950s archive, I had some pages photocopied. Later I presented my brother with his 1950s "criminal record" – an unconventional Christmas present. A typical entry reads: "Insolent in class. Two on the hand".

The very fact that one could be caned *was* a deterrent to bad behaviour, at least in my case. Certain other features of 1950s school life were disagreeable. I hated school milk, but made a show of drinking from the small bottle handed to me by the class "Milk Monitor". Milk bottles for the classroom held one-third of a pint. There were no fridges, of course, and milk soon curdled on a warm Summer's day. The leftovers in the bottles soon turned, leaving the classroom with a slightly cheesy odour.

Free school milk was first introduced in 1921 and became universal under The School Milk Act of 1946. Ellen Wilkinson, the first woman to hold the post of Minister of Education, succeeded in ensuring that all pupils received their free one-third of a pint. Thank you, Ellen.

A visit by the Nit-Nurse was always exciting, as this meant finding out who was "dirty". Her search for head lice was straightforward. We lined up. When my turn came, the Nit-Nurse investigated my hair with a steel comb. This comb was then dipped in a mug of smelly white disinfectant before being used again on the next child. I never had nits, but some kids did. They were told to move off to one side and wait. I never stayed around long enough to find out what they were waiting for.

This was at a time when hair was washed only once a week (or perhaps at much longer intervals). There was an attitude of indifference in some families; parents would say to themselves: "Well, I had nits when I was a kid and so did everyone else. We're still here!"

---ooo---

At the age of 10 I noticed that the school routine was changing. It became increasingly geared towards the 11-Plus exam that marked the completion of Infant and Junior education. The 11-Plus, established by The Education Act 1944, largely determined a child's future. A pass meant entry into a Grammar School and access to an academic education leading to O-Levels and A-Levels. Failure meant attendance at a less academic Secondary Modern School. Around 75 per cent of pupils failed the 11-Plus and went to Secondary Moderns, which provided a vocational education. This system was black and white – pass or fail. As exam day approached, Mum frequently uttered her comforting saying: "You can only do your best".

The 11-Plus exam's three main elements were arithmetic, essay-writing and general problem-solving. I found the lead-in to the 11-Plus quite straightforward. We had homework tasks and revision sheets. These were perfect for getting down to problem-solving and handling simple maths with fractions. I was well aware of the exam's significance but I don't recall feeling stressed. Many children *were* worried, but it wasn't meant to be that way. The original idea was straightforward: to identify the form of education best suited to each child. Unfortunately, the 11-Plus system became dominated by competition to get into the top Grammar schools, as opposed to meeting individual educational needs in the most appropriate way. Mum and Dad were pleased when I passed. I left them to it and went to the park, to play football. After all, it was the start of the Summer break.

---oOo---

During my childhood I was never one for sporting heroes, although some names still resonate down the years. They include Argentina's Juan-Manuel Fangio, perhaps the world's greatest racing driver. Just the mention of his name conjures up an image of raw courage, with death always close at hand. His British counterpart, Stirling Moss, was greatly admired. He raced from 1948 to 1962 and won 212 of his 529 races. He retired after a near fatal crash which left him in a coma for a month. Stirling Moss always preferred to race in British cars, once commenting: "Better to lose honourably in a British car than win in a foreign one."

Stirling Moss was knighted in 2000, an award that recognised his motor-racing achievements and reflected his enormous popularity. He was responsible for that cliché, uttered by countless policemen when pulling over speeding motorists: "Who do you think you are, Stirling Moss?"

I was never interested in football teams and personalities, but for some reason remember Nat Lofthouse, who played for *Bolton Wanderers* throughout his career. He was English Footballer of the Year in 1953 and retired from the game in 1960 due to injury. He became President of *Bolton Wanderers* in 1986 and received an OBE in 1994.

---oOo---

A handful of Lee Manor pupils with exceptional 11-Plus results were accepted by the area's top Grammar Schools: primarily Roan and Colfe's. I was thought of as rather bright at Lee Manor. I soon discovered that plenty of new pupils at Roan School were just as smart and, in some cases, a good deal smarter. Roan was a serious Grammar school, founded in 1677. It had a motto: *Honore et labore* (*"With honour and hard work"*). It had traditions, an esteemed founder (John Roan, "Yeoman of Harriers" to King Charles I) and a phalanx of stern teachers. One, in particular, had a skull-like appearance. Dan Dare's *Mekon* might have been his brother. This gowned figure of authority smoked endless *Du Maurier* cigarettes.

The entrance interview for Roan was daunting. Accompanied by my mother, I passed through the school's wrought iron gates in Maze Hill, Greenwich, and gazed up at the building's attractive cupola. It was surmounted by a gilded stag, the school's emblem, derived from John Roan's coat-of-arms. We were ushered into the presence of Mr W. L. Garstang, the Headmaster (1959—74). He was a tall, gaunt figure in black gown and mortar board. His looks belied his manner, which was pleasant and interested. I was accepted.

Whilst at Grammar school (Roan and others) I witnessed occasional savage behaviour by teachers with short fuses and violent tendencies. It was common to throw chalk about. One or two also threw the heavy blackboard "dusters", seeking a painful strike on the heads of offenders. I recall one particularly spiteful teacher fond of using his open hand, delivering vicious blows across the back of the head. There was also a teacher who delighted in beating boys on the bottom. This punishment was administered in the changing room, using a large gym shoe. Much later in life I was told that this man had been convicted of sexual offences against boys.

---oOo---

Empire Day became unacceptable when the British Empire disappeared. It was rebranded "British Commonwealth Day" in 1958. Even this was not enough for the politically correct. By 1966 it was "Commonwealth Day". The traditional playground celebrations were only a memory. It is sobering to find the toys of your childhood on sale at antique fairs. It is certainly distressing to find that an event you once took part in, as a child, is now the subject of historical re-enactment! In recent years the Beamish Museum, near Chester-Le-Street, has held Empire Day celebrations in May. Commonwealth Day, meanwhile, has moved from 24 May to 11 June, the Queen's official birthday.

---oOo---

In 2006 the regulator OFSTED declared Lee Manor, in its 21st-century manifestation, to be a good school with "very good leadership". The school's Internet profile states: "The team agreed with us that we are an inclusive school; that the standards children reach are good, our pupils enjoy their learning and are good at working together." This school takes pride in its achievements, even if its standards of punctuation leave something to be desired.

OFSTED described racial harmony within the school as "quite remarkable". Around three-quarters of pupils are white. Lee Manor today is bigger than most primary schools, with over 400 pupils, yet the average class size, at 28, is slightly smaller than that of the 1950s. The premises now show signs of age, with leaking roofs and poor classroom acoustics. There is no Empire Day but today's pupils have Internet links with schools in other countries, to increase their understanding of the global community. Lee Manor now serves children from three to 11 and its curriculum has elements which were absent from that of the 1950s. It includes "sex and relationship education, drugs education and healthy living". What would Miss White and Miss Williams have made of that?

Perhaps naively, I was shocked when I visited the school in 2005 and found the gates bolted. I was obliged to use the intercom to announce myself. The playground is a weird sight to a pupil of 1950s vintage. It is full of multicoloured murals and strange steel palm trees. Apparently, today's pupils can become involved in the hiring of teachers! They may be asked to think up questions, to be put at a new teacher's interview. They might even meet prospective candidates for senior posts. What would Mr Herbert have made of that? The very thought would have made his *Trilby* fall off! And God only knows what Mr Leale would have made of pupils chatting away and texting on their mobile phones during the school day. In the 1950s I carried no personal items to school, other than a small model racing car (a *Vanwall*) and my rocket-shaped cap bomb – both hidden deep in my pockets. I had no rucksack, mobile phone or ipod.

No "Spitfires", no British Bulldog: Lee Manor School's modern playground, with its murals and steel palm trees.

As for sex education, the big change came in the 1970s, with the introduction of specific curriculum elements concerned with human reproduction and contraception. The pace of change quickened in the 1980s, with the feminists demanding teaching on gender inequality issues. Other elements have been added to deal with relationships and parenting. Everything was thrown into confusion (some might say panic) with the arrival of HIV/AIDS. Sex education became an over-cooked stew of disease prevention, attempts to contain soaring numbers of under-16 pregnancies and demands for more action on gender inequality and gay rights. Sex education and the sexual health of minors is now a legal minefield. Cases have tested whether parents have a right to know if their children have been given contraception (with the parents discovering that their rights are very limited). Today's enlightened schools encourage pupils to discuss the most intimate matters, such as how to maximise sexual pleasure. We have moved a long way from the amoeba, tadpoles and frogs, gametes and zygotes.

Nothing better illustrates the collective stupidity of Government and zealots than the war with parents over confidentiality and the provision of contraception to minors. During 2012 it was reported that 1,700 girls aged 13 and 14 were fitted with contraceptive implants and another 800 had injections (also providing contraception, but for a shorter period). The parents were not informed, even *after* the event (unless the children themselves decided to tell them). Parents challenging these actions have lost in court and in the House of Lords.

The number of girls aged 15 and under given long-term contraception more than doubled in the five years to 2011 (from 2,900 to 7,400). The policy dimwits are mesmerised by Britain's appalling teenage pregnancy rate – double that of France and Germany. They believe the best way forward is to keep parents out of the loop and to provide contraception for more under-age girls. No thought is given as to how this might actually *increase* the sexualisation of minors. This, in turn, *increases* the spread of sexually transmitted diseases such as Chlamydia. It is thought that around one in three girls have sex at 15 years or younger.

---ooo---

Talks about how to obtain and heighten orgasm might be acceptable in today's classrooms but the Nit-Nurse is banned, out of place in a progressive school environment. The Nit-Nurse disappeared during the 1990s, as hair examinations were "embarrassing and humiliating". Instead, today's parents receive a leaflet on *pediculus humanus capitus*, the human head louse. This is not an attractive creature;

it is about the size of a match head, with six legs and claws – equipment evolved specifically to live on human head hair.

Responsibility for head lice control has passed from schools to parents. Under the 1996 Education Act, parents failing in their responsibilities are guilty of an offence, should repeated infection with head lice occur as a result of neglect. There might be almost universal access to the bath or shower (and any number of treatments available from the chemist), yet outbreaks of head lice remain common in schools. Children with head lice are sent home. This must be "embarrassing and humiliating" for the kids concerned.

---ooo---

The 1950s approach to discipline and punishment would now be regarded as abusive, to the point where the teachers involved might well acquire a criminal record. Yet, even today, corporal punishment has a surprisingly large number of advocates. They argue that it is immediate, efficient and does not interfere with learning (unlike suspension). Others, of course, believe that any form of physical punishment amounts to violence and abuse.

Today, teachers and staff at all British educational establishments are prohibited from inflicting physical punishment on children. Corporal punishment in State schools (and schools part-funded by the State) was banned in 1987. This ban was extended to private schools over the 1999-2003 period. Yet, corporal punishment remains a subject of hot debate amongst parents and teachers. A 2008 *Times Educational Supplement* poll of over 6,000 UK teachers found that one in five supported the cane in extreme cases. There is a public perception that the ban on corporal punishment has contributed to deteriorating behaviour. As for "suspension", critics point out that offenders just tend to regard this as extra holiday.

In 2011 another *TES* survey found that half of parents of Secondary School children and nearly 20 per cent of students supported bringing back the cane (which, it must be said, is an unlikely prospect). Perhaps this reflects the fact that the Department of Education records nearly 1,000 suspensions for abuse and assault *every school day*. As for the very young, in 2011 over 2,000 four and five-year-olds were excluded for disrupting lessons or violent behaviour.

The flogging of pupils is prohibited but, apparently, it is permissible to scare kids to death. In 2012 a Kent Headmaster donned a clown's wig, put on a jumpsuit and, armed with what looked like a gun (in fact, an old water tap), grabbed the School Caretaker. He bundled him into his car and sped off in a staged abduction. Some of the children were scared, thinking that what they had seen was real. In fact, this abduction was a "role-playing" teaching exercise, designed to stimulate riveting eye-witness accounts by pupils. This was not the first dramatic role-play of its type. Teachers have, for example, simulated the landing of alien spaceships! One school traumatised pupils by staging an incident in which a teacher was "shot dead". I am sure Mr Herbert would have administered "six of the best" to all teachers involved in such japes. If this is the only way they can secure an interesting school essay from pupils, perhaps they should consider another career.

---oOo---

School meals have always generated controversy. Local Education Authorities first received powers to provide free school meals when The Education Act 1906 became law. In the 1950s children from "poor families" received free school meals. Things are more complicated under today's regime: "Children whose parents receive Income Support; income-based Job Seekers' Allowance; support under Part IV of the Immigration and Asylum Act 1999; or Child Tax Credit, but who are not entitled to Working Tax Credit and whose annual income (as assessed by the Inland Revenue) that from 6 April 2005 does not exceed £13,910; or the Guaranteed Element of State Pension Credit are entitled to free school meals."

Whether they pay or not, what do today's pupils actually get for their school dinners? Those who do pay hand over £2 for a meal (5p in the 1950s). In May 2012 a nine-year-old became an Internet sensation when she posted images of two school meals. The pressed plastic trays had plenty of space for the meagre fare. One meal consisted of a greyish-looking cheeseburger with two potato croquettes, a few limp slices of cucumber and an ice lolly. The second meal involved a tired slice of pizza with a sprinkling of sweet corn and a lonely potato croquette, supported by a small cupcake for dessert. It seems celebrity chef Jamie Oliver's campaign for quality school food has failed to reach the east coast of Scotland, at least the area where this young whistleblower lives. The school responded by banning photography in the lunch break. The campaigner retaliated by writing a blog which went on to raise enough money to build a school meals facility for several thousand African children.

Perhaps the packed lunch is the answer. The Food Standards Agency offers "lunchbox ideas". Presumably, children living close to the school can no longer go home to lunch, as the streets are dangerous, the home is empty during the day and the food in the fridge is likely to be the same cheap junk on offer at school.

---oOo---

The 11-Plus exam was redesigned in the 1960s, along the lines of an IQ test. Today, it lingers on in some parts of the country – an entrance examination for a small population of surviving Grammar schools.

Exams, *per se*, remain a political minefield, following decades of "dumbing down" and a relatively recent, hamfisted attempt to shift into reverse in the subject of English. Old-fashioned O-Levels and CSEs (Certificates of Secondary Education) were merged, as GCSEs, in 1988. AS Levels (some based on just one year of study) sit alongside dumbed down A-Levels. Today's exams are almost impossible to fail and, consequently, carry little weight as qualifications.

Roan became a comprehensive in 1983. Colfe's fared better, as a co-educational independent day school.

Meanwhile, the dead hand of "enlightenment" continues to slap education in the face. During 2012 an MP called for a debate on a ludicrous rule he had uncovered in one of his constituency's schools. The teachers had been told not to correct more than three spelling errors at a time, as red ink discourages children.

There is no shortage of fresh, loony ideas. One recent brainwave is to provide "anger management lessons" for pre-school toddlers. Nurseries are to spot suitable cases for treatment. The plan is to send the more difficult infants to specialised nurseries. From five upwards, disruptive children would be placed in "Pupil Referral Units". New teachers would be encouraged to gain experience in Pupil Referral Units. And so it goes on...

---oOo---

- 4 -

"Get on and put your feet in there"

··

A decade of change transformed fashion as the austere 1940s gave way to the more colourful 1950s. The "screen goddesses" dictated ladies' fashion, bringing in tiny waistlines, wide belts and full skirts. This did much for the sale of corsets and "corselettes" (a corset/bra combination). Conical bras turned young women into Boudica lookalikes.

There were new materials, such as nylon and acrylic polyester. Some of these clothes were said not to crease or require ironing. There was a new and vibrant teenage market. Films, particularly *Rebel Without a Cause* (1955) and *The Wild One* (1953), created the jeans, white T-shirt and black leather jacket look. Rock and roll propelled teenage fashion, the most obvious result being the Teddy Boy styling of drainpipe trousers, long jackets and "Winklepicker" pointed shoes or thick, crepe-soled "brothel-creepers". Young girls favoured brightly coloured full skirts or jeans, with tight blouses or sweaters. What a time to be alive!

Sadly, all this excitement passed me by. I had yet to reach my teenage years. I had no interest in fashion, although I did like the look of American-style baseball boots. My wardrobe was utilitarian; our family budget had no room for fashion.

---ooo---

Some of my clothes came from Pasold, makers of the famous *Ladybird* range of clothing for children up to the age of 13. These clothes were sold by independent retailers under the *Ladybird* label, or under own brand labels by the likes of Marks and Spencer and British Home Stores.

Ladybird was the most popular brand of children's clothes during the 1950s. Pasold had an amazing history. It was founded 300 years ago by Johannes George Pasold, who championed new technology, in the form of looms and knitting machines. His base was in Fleissen, Czechoslovakia. In modern times, the garments were sold throughout Europe but the *Ladybird* label was launched only in the UK.

By the 1930s Fleissen was a problem – thanks to the Nazis the Sudetenland was not the best place to be! Applying Johannes' principles of smart thinking,

Pasold built a new base in Britain and opened a long, fruitful relationship with Woolworth's and other British stores. When Hitler took over the Sudetenland, the manufacturers of *Ladybird* garments were secure at their new Home Counties headquarters, at Langley. The company prospered, supplying major British retailers. Meanwhile, the Fleissen plant made Wehrmacht uniforms (without the *Ladybird* label).

Most of my clothes came from Marks and Spencer (a happy tradition that continues to this day). I did have a few special items. Aunty Ivy was a gifted knitter and produced amazing Fair Isle sweaters in bright, complex designs. I was less impressed with her "cute" Fair Isle berets (although, today, I am proud to have an example in my small store of 1950s treasures).

My favourite item was the "star jumper", dark blue and covered in small white stars. I had no sense of dress at the tender age of six, but refused to be parted from my star jumper and wore it as often as possible. I also liked my yellow Cub tie, with its small wolf's head motif. It looked very fetching when partnered with an otherwise dull grey v-neck pullover.

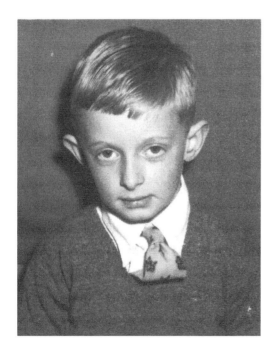

Looking smart: the author with yellow Cub tie.

All boys wore short trousers until entering secondary school at 11. My short, grey trousers were held up by another treasured possession – a snake belt. The ends of this colourful elasticated belt were brought together by two interlocking silver, s-shaped lugs. Every boy had a snake belt. The unattractive sight of my thin white legs was eased by long grey woollen socks. They were turned over at the top, just below the knees, and kept up by elasticated bands. For most of the year I wore sandals of a reddish brown leather, with designs cut into the top.

Going to a 1950s shoe shop was an adventure. In one corner, beside the racks of shoe-boxes, was the X-ray machine known to the trade as the "Pedascope", or "Shoe-fitting Fluoroscope". I was happy to obey when told: "Get on and put your feet in there". It was wonderful! I peered into the visor and saw the bones of my feet! It was incredible to see them move as I wiggled my toes. The shop assistant then peered into the visor, to check for size. Mum was invited to check there was enough room at the toes. Meanwhile, my feet were cooked by the machine! God knows how much radiation I received; no wonder these machines were quietly withdrawn within a few years. Later, I came to appreciate that the X-ray source was in the base of the machine and fired upwards, through the feet and, presumably, also through the genitals.

As for other footwear, I hated the black plimsolls we wore for games. They gave no comfort or protection. I was happy to see my pair chewed by Nell, our black and tan mongrel dog.

My kneecaps, visible between sock-tops and short trouser bottoms, were often covered with grazes and scabs from multiple falls in the playground. I was always told not to pick the scabs, otherwise my legs would fester. "Festering" sounded very unpleasant and I tried to ignore the scabs, which itched dreadfully.

It was common for schoolboys to wear caps. I also carried a brown leather school satchel, its colour matching the sandals on my irradiated feet. The satchel's contents included a *Pac-a-Mac*, tightly folded into a small bundle. This was a lightweight, full length raincoat made of thin, smelly grey plastic. It could be rolled into a very small shape (if you had the patience). The *Pac-a-Mac* fought to keep its folds and creases. It was difficult to put on and the buttons – recessed discs of slightly firmer plastic – had to be gouged out of their recesses. The *Pac-a-Mac* kept out the rain but made its owner sweat copiously. I preferred my black, belted mac – no great shakes in the fashion department but infinitely better than its plastic counterpart.

I looked forward to Fridays and "Cub Night". I wore my Cub uniform to school: the cap with its central metal star, a green sweater with an armful of badges, scarf held in place by a fur "woggle" and a lanyard and whistle. As a "Sixer", that whistle recognised my rank.

During the late 1950s I became aware of fashion. I never owned a black leather jacket, but I did persuade Mum to buy me a black zip-up windcheater. This looked almost "cool" with the collar turned up. I now cut a very different figure from the nine-year-old in his Cub uniform! Winklepicker shoes came in but my parents refused to budge. Winklepickers were for yobs! Fashion moved on. The innovations included "Chelsea Boots" – high-sided shoes, elasticated at the ankle and with extended, squared-off toes. I still wanted baseball boots and eventually got a pair (probably just to shut me up).

Mum's wardrobe included skirts and dresses with wide belts and in bright floral prints. When working around the house she wore a "pinny", a floral pinafore overall. Her clothes (with the exception of the "pinny") were very different from those of the war years and the age of *Utility*. In the 1940s, women's clothes were less feminine, being square cut and severe. At that time Mum's favourite outfit had been a two-piece suit in a smart Prince of Wales check, with pronounced, square-cut shoulders. She acquired this at the tender age of 18; it must have made her feel very grown up.

Dad made do with a very limited 1950s wardrobe. He had few clothes which might now be described as "casual". He had a couple of suits, a few shirts and ties, several pairs of grey flannels, a couple of button-up sweaters (including one with the ubiquitous mock leather buttons) and a belted mac finished in a peculiar shade of RAF blue. He wore warm long johns for night work on the track. He always wore a vest, but never, to my recollection, a string vest. He was almost always dressed in a jacket, white shirt and tie, even at weekends. In the garden he wore an old jumper and trousers from a worn-out suit. His jet black hair was always combed back with a crisp parting. It shone with a liberal sprinkling of *Cusson's Brilliantine*.

---ooo---

Pasold, the originators of *Ladybird*, merged with Coats, Paton and Baldwin in 1965. The Langley factory fell behind the times and the brand declined. Nevertheless, in 1984 Woolworth's sought exclusive UK rights to *Ladybird*. Eventually, the *Ladybird* label appeared in Woolworth's stores. In 2000, *Ladybird* was sold outright to Woolworth's, but this famous High Street name went into Administration during the disastrous "Credit Crunch" eight years later. Shop Direct rescued Woolworth's and the *Ladybird* name; the famous garments are now available on-line. As for the shoe shops, X-ray machines are history and little talked about. They seem to have done me no long term harm; my feet (and the rest) are still attached.

---ooo---

− 5 −

Germoline, Zubes and Fear of Polio

My parents grew up in fear of infectious disease. Tuberculosis, Diphtheria and Scarlet Fever were killers. These threats had receded by the 1950s, but infections that crippled and killed children were still around. Polio was dreaded.

Common ailments were sorted out over-the-counter at the chemists. Grazes from playground falls were smeared with *Germolene*, then a thick, violently pink ointment with a pungent smell of antiseptic. It was invented by Sir Henry Veno, of cough mixture fame. I preferred *Zam-Buk* for grazed knees. For some reason I loved that name. *Zam-Buk* was an old-fashioned mix of beeswax, eucalyptus oil, camphor, red thyme and pine. It originated in South Africa and developed a loyal following worldwide.

I was happy to have a sore throat or cough if that meant I could eat *Zubes*. I preferred them to most boiled sweets! Now made in "original" and honey and lemon, I still find the originals (menthol and aniseed oil) hard to beat. They were promoted by a delightful jingle: "Zubes! Zubes! Zubes are good for your tubes!"

Every child in 1950s Britain loathed Cod Liver Oil, usually dispensed in flabby gelatine capsules. I would have hated it more had I known it was made by topping up a barrel of cod livers with seawater and leaving it to ferment for up to a year! Today, Cod Liver Oil is prized for its Omega-3 fatty acids, which benefit the heart and circulatory system and ease arthritis. The 1950s child, however, received the oil for its vitamin content – especially Vitamin D, for sound skeletal development. Fifty years earlier, Cod Liver Oil had been used to treat malnourished children with Rickets. Some experts now argue that Cod Liver Oil is *too rich* in Vitamin A and Vitamin D and that it is better for children to get their Omega-3 oils by eating fish. Equally, it has been suggested that lack of Omega-3 in a child's diet contributes to learning difficulties and attention-related problems. Perhaps there are good reasons for re-introducing Cod Liver Oil!

Rose Hip Syrup was more agreeable. The fresh fruit shortage during World War Two prompted a campaign to encourage the public to pick wild rose hips. Rose Hip Syrup is rich in Vitamin C. Autumn hip collectors walked the lanes and supplied the raw material for millions of bottles of syrup. Rose Hip Syrup continued to be made during the years of austerity after the war.

---ooo---

Feeling "one degree under" meant a visit to the doctors. Our surgery was at nearby Hither Green. Nan still talked in awed terms of "Dr Summerskill". Dr William Summerskill had the practice in 1913—14. He was the father of Dr (later, Baroness) Edith Summerskill, who became one of Labour's most distinguished MPs. Young Edith saw real squalor whilst accompanying her father on his home visits. A deep social conscience was awakened and forged a formidable MP, Minister and social campaigner. Edith played a crucial role in the birth of the National Health Service.

Memories of another much-loved Doctor at Hither Green were still fresh in the minds of patients in the 1950s. During the war years, the practice was held by two Irish brothers, Drs Edward and Patrick Carey. "Dr Pat" had been killed whilst making his rounds during the Blitz. My memories are of Dr. Tangney, a kindly, interested man. He was polite, unhurried and always eager to enquire about the rest of the family. There was no computer on his desk, just a stethoscope.

I found his Surgery a gloomy place. There was no appointments system. The large waiting room was filled with two double rows of hard chairs placed back to back, each leading to a consulting room door. It was always a very long wait, shuffling along from chair to chair, reaching the end of the line and turning through 180 deg. for the "home straight". I tried to ignore the sick, who coughed and spluttered around us. If we were not ill when we arrived at the Surgery, we certainly were when we left! Looking back, across the years, that waiting room seems crowded and unhygienic. I remember staring at two large golden cherubs, mounted on the wall. Perhaps they represented children who had died during their long wait to see the Doctor?

A visit to the Doctors was much preferred to a visit to the Dentist. The rubber mask supplying gas smelt vile. I always made an effort to be brave when visiting Baring Road Dental Surgery. When it was over, I felt dizzy and could taste blood in my mouth. For those fascinated by trivia, nitrous oxide was first used by a Dentist in 1844. Some years earlier, those moving in fashionable circles had held "laughing gas parties" – all the rage in the early 19th-century. It seems that the search for a "high" is nothing new, although I don't recall feeling euphoric after a dose of dental gas.

Going to the hospital was even worse. Lewisham Hospital looked like a prison. It took in cholera victims from 1867 and "lunatics" from 1897. I managed to avoid that hospital, beyond one night under observation for a suspected "grumbling appendix". I did all the grumbling. There were also a few brief calls to Lewisham Hospital for minor injuries and, of course, visits to family members and friends. Most of my family died in Lewisham Hospital. This was more an accident of geography than any reflection on its standards of care (although, today, those standards are often challenged on websites). Back in the 1950s I was more concerned about Lewisham Hospital's gigantic chimney, which dominated the site. I was convinced that people who died in the hospital were "sent up the chimney". Much later in life it occurred to me that, as a small child, I must have seen news coverage of the Nazi death camps, so prompting a reasonable assumption that tall chimneys were to be avoided at all costs.

---ooo---

Every now and then a boil appeared on my slim young neck. Mum was particular in matters of hygiene but, in the 1950s, Friday night was bath night. That was it until next Friday! During the rest of the week it was a matter of a "cat's lick" with a flannel, standing at the scullery sink. As that red spot on my neck grew larger Nan muttered the dreaded word "poultice!" Today, pharmacies sell under-the-tongue sprays to clear up boils. The 1950s solution, the poultice, was more dramatic. It was applied red-hot, to draw out the pus. This was painful but, in all probability, less painful than "lancing".

I caught most of the common childhood diseases, including Chicken Pox and Measles. Until a vaccine was developed, in 1963, Measles was the world's most infectious agent. There were 135 million cases annually in the developing world, resulting in six million deaths. Measles, with its blotchy red rash, still kills around one million children every year. Infection confers lifelong immunity, but this is little comfort if you happen to be one of the unfortunates developing respiratory complications, leading to pneumonia.

During 1956, in bed and feverish with Measles, I became convinced that the world would end unless I finished reciting my entire "times tables" without stumbling. Measles killed around 500 British children every year in the 1950s. There were up to 800,000 cases annually and every child got it at some point. German Measles, or Rubella, was milder than Measles but caused a similar rash. Rubella is a major threat to the foetus, causing severe abnormalities. I had my fair share of colds and flu. There was an "Asian Flu" pandemic in 1957.

Our parents knew how swiftly disease can take young lives. Their childhood years had been overshadowed by Scarlet Fever, once a prolific child-killer. All children in a family could be wiped out within a few weeks. There were major urban epidemics in the 19th-century and Scarlet Fever became the most common infectious cause of death among children. Two of Charles Dickens' children died of Scarlet Fever. This disease took on a milder form from the 1880s and was rare by the 1950s, although it was still much talked about. My generation had every reason to be grateful for Scarlet Fever's decline. Symptoms included "Strep Throat", followed by chills, aches, poor appetite and vomiting. Toxins could produce circulatory failure and death. The red rash looked like sunburn and the skin and tongue peeled. Within a few weeks Rheumatic Fever might take hold and damage the heart.

Diphtheria was a disease anyone would be happy to miss. Immunisation had begun early in World War Two and it had been almost eliminated by the 1950s. Diphtheria spread from person to person by droplet infection. It attacked the upper air passages, formed a leathery deposit and produced a harsh cough, fever and neck swelling (which could lead to breathing difficulties and, eventually, asphyxia). Toxins could attack the nervous system and cause paralysis. Heart failure was the most common cause of death from Diphtheria and children in the 2 - 10 age range were most at risk.

Whooping cough was equally unpleasant. Coughing fits could last for six weeks before abating. The name comes from the high-pitched "whoop" made when babies and children inhale after coughing. Vaccination began in the 1950s. Today, case numbers are low although there was a surge in 2011, with over 1,000 laboratory-confirmed cases. Complications can include Pneumonia and seizures or brain damage.

Mumps, another potentially serious complaint, results in swollen salivary glands, headaches, fatigue and fever. Mumps can lead to inflammation of the brain, swelling of the pancreas and deafness. Men contracting Mumps after puberty may suffer painful swelling of the testicles. Mumps is still around; there was an outbreak in Britain in 2004.

People still feared Tuberculosis in the 1950s. TB, or "Consumption", is spread primarily by inhalation and anyone caring for a victim is at greatly increased risk. The childhood stage produces fever and poor appetite. The disease can surface in later life as Pulmonary TB, with its characteristic cough and bloody sputum. "Galloping Consumption" can take hold, resulting in the destruction of the bronchial tube linings and death. TB held the 19th-century urban poor in a savage grip. The BCG vaccination did not confer full protection but TB was in retreat after World War Two. Yet, TB cases began to increase in Britain and other Western nations during the 1980s. TB is still around!

---oOo---

Polio was the 1950s bogeyman. Polio-crippled child beggars were a common sight on British city streets in the early 20th-century. Many victims were shut away in hospitals and institutions. There were severe Polio epidemics in the 1880s and "Summer plagues" of Polio became frequent after 1910. In 1947 an upsurge of Polio brought British parents close to panic. There were 8,000 cases – 10 times the annual average – and high rates of Polio continued into the 1950s. In severe cases victims are unable to breathe unassisted. Entire wards were filled with "iron lungs" that kept the occupants alive (at least for a time). Many sufferers, including my Nan, had an arm or a leg permanently paralysed or wasted by Polio.

Fortunately, the Salk and Sabin vaccines of the 1950s proved effective and Polio was much reduced by the 1960s. There is still no cure for Polio and treatment can involve prolonged rehabilitation, braces, corrective shoes and, in some instances, surgery. Today, Polio is rare in Western countries but it remains endemic in Nigeria, Pakistan and Afghanistan. The Americas were declared free of Polio by 1994 and Europe was free by 2002.

Polio may have been the most dreaded disease, but it was a boy in a wheelchair who terrified me in the 1950s. At that time I hadn't heard of Hydrocephalus, or "Water on the Brain", but the sight of that poor boy – with his huge, misshapen head – made me wonder if the same fate could befall me. I assumed he had been punished for telling a really big lie and I decided to try to be more honest.

Hydrocephalus is an abnormal build-up of fluid within the cranial cavity. In the past, babies and children with this condition either died or were placed in institutions. Today's treatment involves surgical insertion of a "shunt", diverting fluid from the head. Without treatment, Hydrocephalus results in loss of coordination, seizures, learning difficulties and crossed eyes. I can still picture that tiny figure in his wheelchair, the large, bulging head wobbling on his small frame. His mother had plenty of courage and love; she pushed that wheelchair and ignored the stares. Fifty years on, children with Hydrocephalus who live in poor countries still die, as their parents lack the money for shunt surgery.

---oOo---

Within the space of 60 years immunisation has transformed public health in Britain. Diphtheria, Whooping Cough, Measles and Polio have been vanquished. Today, British babies are immunised against many diseases, followed by more immunisation (including the "MMR" – Measles, Mumps, Rubella) at around 12 months. There are pre-school "boosters" and a combined injection for Tetanus, Diphtheria and Polio in the teenage years. Adults – primarily the elderly and high risk groups – receive "flu jabs" and immunisation against Pneumococcus, responsible for Pneumonia and Meningitis. The BCG is given to babies living in areas with high TB rates. Young children with parents and grandparents born in countries with a high incidence of TB also receive the BCG. Prior to 2005, all UK schoolchildren received the BCG at around 13 years of age. This is no longer thought necessary, given the low TB rates in many parts of the UK.

In February 1998 *The Lancet* published a notorious study linking the MMR with autism. Later, it declared that it should not have published the paper. By that stage, the early 1990s MMR rate of over 90 per cent had fallen to 80 per cent. Subsequent studies found no link between MMR and autism. The MMR take-up has recovered slowly (back to 88 per cent in 2011), but it still remains too low to confer "herd immunity".

In 2008 the Health Protection Agency warned that, once again, Measles was endemic in the population. The numbers of unvaccinated children are sufficient to sustain the virus. The finger of blame points to the MMR controversy; concerned parents have long memories! This sorry tale undermined a major public health achievement in 1994, when Measles ceased to be endemic in the UK.

---ooo---

Looking beyond the MMR fiasco, immunisation amounts to a huge public health victory. In 1940, prior to vaccination, there were over 400,000 cases of Measles, nearly 21,000 cases of Mumps and over 24,000 cases of Rubella. In 1997, following decades of vaccination, the numbers had fallen to 186, 175 and 99 respectively. Diphtheria cases fell from over 46,000 to four and Polio from more than 1,000 to zero. This is the legacy of the vision that established the National Health Service in 1948, just six months before I was born. People no longer lived in fear of being unable to pay for medical treatment. The State controlled an infrastructure capable of delivering effective national vaccination programmes.

Unfortunately, the NHS is now exposed to the vagaries of fashion, including attempts to combine self-help and modern communications. We are in the age of "health apps", which aim to reduce unnecessary visits to surgeries and hospitals.

Cancer patients, Diabetes sufferers and those with heart and lung conditions are to be encouraged to take daily measurements and "text" them to a centralised point. Oxygen levels, blood pressure and other readings will be analysed and participating patients will receive texts offering advice and guidance.

The NHS today is a hungry explorer, stumbling through a dense jungle of bright ideas. It is possible that fewer cases of sudden deterioration – followed by A&E admission – may result from this new initiative. Yet the approach would further segregate patient and doctor. It also assumes that the elderly and sick are keen to text. How would the health professionals cope with this tidal wave of routine data? Who would be accountable when dangerous readings go undetected? Who has the time to monitor the monitors?

---oOo---

The smell of coal smoke defined the 1950s. Dependence on coal amounted to a major public health threat. London's "Great Smog" killed thousands in December 1952, presenting the fledgling NHS with a huge challenge. Coal consumption soared during a severe cold snap. A temperature inversion trapped smoke and factory fumes, producing smog (smoke and fog). It developed on 5 December and stayed for five days. Londoners accustomed to "pea-soupers" realised that this was something different. People on the Isle of Dogs could not see their own feet. There were reports that cattle at Smithfield Market were choking to death. The thick, yellowish smog increased the death rate by over 4,000 (and perhaps as many as 8,000 more died in the following weeks). Most victims were already suffering from respiratory illness.

The pollutant load under the inversion layer was estimated at 1,000 tonnes of smoke particles, 2,000 tonnes of carbon dioxide, 140 tonnes of hydrochloric acid and 370 tonnes of sulphur dioxide (which became 800 tonnes of sulphuric acid). Parliament took action, introducing the Clean Air Act of 1956. There was another Clean Air Act in 1968. By the late 1960s the smell of the 1950s had disappeared, thanks to smokeless fuels.

It took time for the 1956 Act to take effect. In 1962 around 750 Londoners died of smog exposure. In the late 1950s I quite liked the eerie world of smog-filled streets. It really was a yellowish colour, swirling around street lamps and producing glowing spheres of fumes. It was extremely hard to find your way about. Yet, the smog made an over-familiar environment seem new, strange and exciting. It made me cough but no-one told me not to go out!

---oOo---

– 6 –

Broken Biscuits and Camp Coffee

Early British experiments in self-service shopping were novel enough to make headlines in 1949. The pioneers included the Co-op. Until then British shoppers queued for service from counter assistants and the assistant, rather than the customer, did the picking. In food shops and large stores, such as Woolworths and Marks and Spencer, produce and goods were on display but handling was strictly the business of assistants. Each counter had its cash till.

There were no plastic carrier bags. Housewives took their own shopping bags or baskets. They shopped for a day or two, rather than a week. There were no cars to load. If the weight of shopping exceeded carrying capacity, wicker baskets on wheels were used. Many stores delivered shopping but customers were charged for this service.

Early trials in self-service shops were complicated by food rationing, which persisted well into the 1950s. Experimental self-service stores posted notices, explaining the new procedures. The customer could fill a basket with unrationed items, but had to queue at the counter to buy those foods still on ration. Housewives gave the new arrangements a mixed reception. Some disliked the idea of fellow customers coming in, handling foods and putting them back. This was the age of fresh food, with very little pre-packaging, and there was concern about hygiene.

At your service: shop assistants at the ready. The margarines are prominent at the bottom right, with brands including Stork and Echo. The woman in the middle is the author's late mother-in-law, Patricia Boylett. In front of her is a large stack of tinned steak and kidney pies.

---ooo---

Most shopping trips were made on foot, with shoppers taking account of local half-day closing. This varied from town to town but it often fell on a Wednesday afternoon. Careful planning and a shopping list were essential as there was no fridge or freezer at home to keep food fresh. An 11th-century Persian physicist is said to have invented the refrigerated coil. This may be so, but it took some time for refrigeration to reach south-east London. The first domestic fridges were produced in the United States in 1913, with General Electric manufacturing the first popular model in 1927. Home freezers were launched in America in 1940, at a time when the British had other things to worry about.

Housewives understood the challenge of keeping food fresh. They bought little and often. There were no packs of frozen food, no ready meals and no Chinese and Indian take-aways. The only "ready meal" on offer was fish and chips. This inability to refrigerate or freeze was responsible for the High Street's special character. During the mid-1800s, growing urbanisation increased the local demand for fresh foods.

It would be a mistake to regard the 1950s as the "golden age" of shopping. There were no "best before" dates on food. Refrigeration of perishables was minimal, handling was inefficient and hygiene was poor. There was something of the Wild West about food retailing. Regulation was lax and some shopkeepers habitually palmed off bruised and tired produce. The more unscrupulous took all sorts of liberties, including "bulking up" and watering down.

What did we eat in the 1950s? This was a time of low expectations and meals tended to be plain and without frills of any kind. It was rare to eat out. Everything was in the hands of the housewife (with the exception of the occasional Friday night treat of fish and chips). Breakfast for kids was usually a traditional cereal, such as *Weetabix* or *Shredded Wheat*. I disliked both. *Shredded Wheat* reminded me of barbed wire. I preferred toast, thickly spread with *Marmite*. A cooked breakfast was unusual. Butter, bacon and sugar – although off ration by the mid-1950s – were still regarded as luxuries and ingrained habits were hard to break. When we had a cooked breakfast we had one rasher each, not four! There was often butter in the dish, bright yellow and runny in Summer, but there was also margarine (which you were expected to use unless told otherwise). I didn't mind *Summer County* margarine. I was fortunate to miss the wartime *National Margarine*.

School dinners gave most kids a hot midday meal during the week. I went home to lunch as soon as I was able, as I hated the smell and sight of school dinners.

Those gigantic steel containers, filled with boiled-out vegetables, made me heave. The sight of disgusting desserts such as tapioca and semolina, all with a great splodge of tinned jam on top, made the sensitive amongst us want to vomit. School food looked and tasted awful.

Lunch at home was better: egg and chips, spam and beans or toad-in-the-hole. There was little variety but plenty for all. We had cold meat on Monday (the leftovers from the Sunday joint). Occasionally, this meat went into a casserole. Mum stretched the budget with cheap cuts, such as tasty (but fatty) breast of lamb. Everyone's favourite was "best end of neck" – lamb chops stuck together. Dessert, if not stewed apple and custard, might be tinned fruit salad or pineapple with *Carnation* milk. On a fruit salad day I always looked for a couple of grapes and a half cherry or two.

Back from school in the late afternoon, I had my usual tea: two crusty rolls filled with cheddar cheese or corned beef. The crusty rolls of the 1950s were absolutely delicious and nothing like today's equivalent. The first bite produced a shower of dark brown crust crumbs, which could be snacked on afterwards. There was not a lot of fruit at home. It was customary to ask "Please may I have an apple", rather than simply take it and start munching. "Fruit" really meant apples and oranges. More exotic fruits were too expensive unless, at the very top of the season, a glut brought down prices.

What did we drink in the 1950s? Well, I drank orange squash and, occasionally, *Tizer* or other fizzy "pop". The adults drank tea or enjoyed an occasional cup of "coffee" made from *Camp Coffee* liquid (with chicory). Mum had an infrequent small light ale, *Babycham* or "Egg Flip" whilst in the pub. Dad usually drank Brown Ale.

---ooo---

As a young child I assumed that the primary purpose of shopping was to gossip; buying food seemed very much a secondary task. I dreaded "bumping into" one of Mum's friends or a relative. With headscarves firmly tied into place and bored kids shuffling around them, the women began to talk, totally oblivious to the world around them. No-one merely passed the time of day in these circumstances. The idea was to have "a good chin-wag". I stood and waited for the rituals of street corner gossip to be completed. It was better when it rained, as the chit-chat was curtailed. This habit of chatting in the street was ingrained. Fewer women worked at this time and their daily routine was to "pop to the shops". During the war, when the men were away, women had turned to each other for support, encouragement and an opportunity to unburden themselves.

We never bought milk during our shopping trips, as it was delivered to our door every morning. There was a time when milkmen on their rounds filled customers' own jugs, but this changed in 1880, when the Express Dairy became the first British producer of an important American innovation, the milk bottle. During the 1950s the milkman's horse and cart was still around but was being replaced by the electric milk float. This was virtually silent – ideal for early morning deliveries. Sadly, however, milk floats produce no horse dung (prized by gardeners). All milk came in glass bottles – modern, high density polyethylene containers were still many years away.

Mum's last job in the evening was to put out the rinsed empties, which were slotted into a wire-framed holder on the doorstep. A note for the milkman was tucked into one of the bottles. We had ordinary, full-fat milk but you could order the creamier "Gold Top" or the ghastly "Sterilised" (which came in a different shaped bottle, finished with a crimped metal top rather than foil). A small rectangle of plywood was balanced on top of the bottles, to defend them against the beaks of predatory birds. If given the chance, they would peck open the tops and enjoy the cream. As far as I was concerned, the birds were welcome to it. I hated the top of the milk.

During the 1950s it was unusual to buy anything other than milk from the milkman. A few other products, such as butter and sugar, were sold occasionally but were cheaper in the shops. From time to time, Mum bought "orange juice" from the milkman. This also came in glass bottles and was (I believe) pasteurised like the milk. It was delicious, having a distinctive taste, completely free of bitterness and quite different from that of other orange drinks.

I rarely saw our milkman, as he delivered too early in the day. Occasionally, I caught sight of him later, when on the way to school. He wore an untidy uniform: peaked cap, a white jacket or overall, an apron and a bag to collect the money. I never drank milk voluntarily. I preferred to wait for the *Corona* lorry's Friday visit. Occasionally, Mum bought a bottle of "pop" – lemonade, raspberryade or cream soda. The empties were worth tuppence each.

I was content to go shopping with Mum whenever Nan was cooking. The smell was awful. Nan had her own tastes and these Victorian favourites included brawn and "bloaters" – herrings smoked with their guts still in (they got their name due to a tendency to swell up during cooking). I understand that bloaters are now regarded as a delicacy (but not by me). Nan also made stews – mostly mutton stew

– flavoured with "Curry Powder", a mix of spices which turned everything a dull orange-brown colour. I hated it.

Children were not permitted to be fussy eaters in the 1950s. Attitudes were different and it was a disgrace to waste food. A child's likes and dislikes counted for little – we really were told to eat up our greens. Any attempt at resistance was met with a blunt warning: we could not "get down" until all plates were cleared. My main concern was to get at the custard. Could I have the skin?

---ooo---

There were several shops close to home, including Clifton's, a tiny general stores on the corner of Hedgley Street and Brightfield Road. This was a small, family-run business. The shelves and small counter displayed almost everything, from lemonade and cheese to tea, sweets and bacon. When Mr and Mrs Clifton died, a daughter – Ruby – took over. Ruby never married. Later, the family pressed Beryl Clifton, Ruby's niece, to run the shop, but they were unsuccessful in their efforts. My Mum had babysat Beryl when she was an infant.

A row of three or four shops stood just yards from Clifton's. They included Kenway's, a cross between a grocers and a hardware store. Mr Kenway, an elderly, kindly man, was rather Dickensian in character. His shop had a peculiar but pleasant smell, a mix of polish, paraffin and dog biscuits. Mr Kenway was very short and his bald, conical head – fringed with a mane of straight, white-grey hair – was just visible beyond the counter. He wore a full length brown overall and peered at customers through round, wire-framed glasses.

The small parade of Lee Green shops that once included Kenway's and Roe's greengrocers: to the far right is Lee High Road and the bridge over the River Quaggy.

Mr Kenway sold paraffin, oil, hardware and dry goods. This is where people without mains electricity picked up their accumulator batteries and gas mantles. Near the door, on the right hand side, stood several open hessian sacks filled with *Spillers' Shapes* dog biscuits. I always looked at these with interest; I was partial to the magnolia-coloured triangular one.

Kenway's had been established for many years. The owner had a well-deserved reputation for friendliness and generosity towards his customers. In the late 1930s Mum's younger brother, Pete, was a particular favourite of Mr Kenway. Pete would be invited to have a go at the "Lucky Dip". He was always sure of a prize, regardless of his luck. Mr Kenway had little in the way of luck in his private life. His wife left him but, fortunately, a friend or relative stepped in to help him. During the 1930s and 1940s, there was often a barrel-organ outside Kenway's, bleating out the day's popular tunes. In the 1950s there was no barrel-organ, just the open doorway revealing those enticing sacks of dog biscuits and a well-swept planked floor. During the winter months the "Chestnut Man" appeared on the corner of Brightfield Road and set up his brazier.

Next door to Kenway's was Rowe's, a greengrocers run by Fred Rowe and his wife. Their shop was a rather scruffy, no-nonsense establishment. Its planked floor was littered with yellowing cabbage leaves. Opposite this small parade was a fish and chip shop. In the 1950s it was an informal Friday night meeting place for teenagers holding "six of chips" (a portion for sixpence, or 2.5p). They propped up a wall, chatted and messed about in a harmless manner. Mum knew this shop as Howlett's. When she was growing up, Howlett's was an unpretentious business, with the fish kept in a big tin bath in the backyard. Twenty-five years later, outside the same shop, my newspaper-wrapped bag of chips was always smothered in salt and vinegar (to the point where vinegar soon began leaking out over my hands).

Lee High Road, connecting Lee Green to Lewisham, was very close. On the corner of Park Lodge, opposite the *Duke of Edinburgh* pub, was Fudge's newsagents and sweet shop. Lee High Road was a challenge; it was busy even then and quite difficult to cross. Fudge's offered four-bar *Kit-Kats* for sixpence. A penny or two went a long way when buying Blackjacks, Flying Saucers, Chews or Milk Gums. I liked Raspberry and Blackberry Drops, sold by the ounce or two ounces. I also liked a peculiar pink sweet, the name of which escapes me. It was long, wafer thin and looked a bit like a solid fireman's ladder. The lattice was brittle and had a strange, semi-liquorice taste.

When Mum went shopping our first target was usually the Home and Colonial – the general stores where my Aunt Vi was Manager. It was counter service only, with plenty of butter, cheese and bacon on display. A vicious-looking bacon slicer made a rather sinister sound as it sliced ham. To the left of the shop doorway was an area for stacked goods, including tins of biscuits. The centre piece of the counter display was a large Cheddar Cheese roundel, cut by a wire equipped with a toggle handle. Butter was taken from a large slab and shaped by wooden paddles.

Home and Colonial, founded in 1883 by tea merchant Julius Drewe, became one of the country's largest food retailers. His wealth paid for Castle Drogo in Devon. Drewe commissioned Lutyens to design Britain's last castle, which was completed just before his death in 1931. Castle Drogo, now a National Trust property, has always been known locally as "Margarine Castle". All Home and Colonial stores had a distinctive shopfront style, with the name displayed in large condensed type.

An off-licence was next to Home and Colonial. I believe this was Victoria Wines. The off-licence was managed by the father of a schoolfriend, Clive Bowman. Clive was the fastest runner I knew. He was very proud of his speed and my Dad took a shine to his cocky, self-assured attitude. One day my 40-year-old Dad (who had been his regiment's cross-country champion) challenged Clive to a race. They tore off down Hedgley Street and my Dad won!

Lee Green also had a Sainsbury's, a shop about the same size as Home and Colonial. Its counters also displayed huge cheese roundels cut by wire, with pieces wrapped up in grease-proof paper. There was also Cave Austin, which was located just off Lee Green's centre, on the road leading to Blackheath. It was not as popular as Sainsbury's or Home and Colonial for food shopping, but it did stock a good range of drink. Shoppers tended to regard it as an off-licence that also sold food.

Several shops sold cheap broken biscuits. These may have been acquired from the Chiltonian biscuit factory, which had moved to a site in nearby Manor Lane after the Great War. I don't remember where the butchers was, but recall the sawdust-covered floor and the reek of old blood. I would stare at the pig's head suspended on a hook, eyeless yet, somehow, still able to stare back at me. I would change position and try to see what a neck looked like when severed. Yuk!

---ooo---

I was no great enthusiast for our frequent shopping trips to Lewisham and its bustling Saturday market. I remember the greengrocers' stalls. Everything was put into paper bags and placed on scales. The bag was then closed by holding it at the corners and twirling it with a deft rotation of the fingers. I enjoy strolling around markets today (especially if they are in the Dordogne).

Lewisham market had its share of dodgy characters. There were the men my Mum called "Spivs". They attracted large audiences with "bargain of a lifetime" claims. Many shoppers stood around enjoying the free entertainment. There were also more furtive traders, selling goods that looked in surprisingly good condition, despite having "fallen off the back of a lorry".

Lewisham's big stores in the 1950s included a large Woolworth's. It had old-fashioned wood-tread escalators. There were cash tills at each counter and every product display had its price tag. One corner of the store was filled with that unmistakable, pungent smell of oil cloth. Chiesmans was a large department store with a reputation for being expensive. Yet its stock was well presented and it sold a lot of furniture. Mum had a good story about Chiesmans. Whenever we walked past the raised area of pavement outside the store, she would tell the story of the shot-down German aircraft that was displayed there during the early war years, to help raise money for the war effort. According to Mum, the traitor "Lord Haw-Haw" (aka William Joyce) – who broadcast for the Germans – worried Lewisham residents when he said that the Luftwaffe was fully aware of this trophy of war and would soon reward the fund-raisers with a return visit! Perhaps this is one of those apocryphal stories that take root in close communities. Yet there may be some truth in it. Nothing pleased Lord Haw-Haw more than to single out towns and cities for highly specific threats.

---oOo---

During the 1950s Mum had a Saturday job in the curtains and nets department of Oxenburghs, the Lewisham store specialising in carpets and soft furnishings. Mum was the first woman to work behind a counter at Oxenburghs. Later, she became very friendly with Connie, the store's second lady assistant. Connie was a Dutch woman who had married an Englishman.

The two Oxenburgh brothers came from an enterprising East European Jewish family. Alec, the younger brother, had a shop in Bromley. Maurice held sway in Lewisham, where, over time, he bought up a row of five small shops where Lee High Road enters the centre of Lewisham. He was successful and the Lewisham store thrived. Alec, however, struggled and Maurice eventually stepped in and employed him. Later, Alec and his family left to make a fresh start in Australia.

Mum always had a good word to say about Maurice Oxenburgh. She remembered his well-groomed white hair and smart suit: "He was always well turned-out". The feelings of respect were mutual. Maurice recognised Mum's ability to put together a good window display. Occasionally, he showed his appreciation by giving her a lift home in his Jaguar. Mum also got on well with George Dimmock, a German manager at the store who had settled in London after the war and married an English girl.

---ooo---

Harold MacMillan's "Winds of change" speech had consequences for the Home and Colonial. In 1961 its name was no longer auspicious. As the Empire continued to shrink, a new identity was required. The Home and Colonial label was dropped for the politically neutral Allied Supplies. The business was acquired in the 1970s by James Goldsmith's Cavenham Foods. In 1982 Allied was taken over by Argyll Foods and a merger with Safeway came five years later. Home and Colonial went the way of Empire.

Today, of course, people do the entire week's shop in the space of an hour and at one location: the supermarket. During that hour, shoppers are unlikely to meet anyone they know and the only conversation will be a response to the question: "Do you want cash back?" Or the shopper can seek out his or her "favourites" on-line and so avoid the stress of that one-line face-to-face conversation at the check-out.

Food retailing giants: the back of Sainsbury's huge store, sprawled across the centre of Lee Green. This elevation confronts the family-run shops of yesteryear.

British High Streets today are in a parlous state. Empty windows and boarded up shopfronts disfigure our towns. Independent shops have been crushed by out-of-town superstores, on-line shopping, new generations who know no better and the catastrophic economic slump which began in 2008. By 2010 around 13 per cent of all High Street shops were vacant. Their loss contributes to the sense of desolation and helplessness pervading most urban areas.

Shoppers today have traded personal service for personal choice. In doing so, they have lost their sense of community. People now rarely gossip in the street. They walk alone, talking into mobiles, texting or plugged in and isolated by "music". They are too busy to stop and talk to each other. The effort and directness of physical contact disturbs them. They prefer to text, twitter and communicate via *Facebook*. They tell each other, electronically, just a little of what they might have told each other face-to-face, 50 years earlier.

In December 2010 a BBC research project cited Lee Green as Britain's most unsuccessful shopping district. Nearly one third (32.34%) of all Lee Green shops were vacant – a higher figure than anywhere else in the country (the average for Greater London was 11.2 per cent). One local paper quoted a shopowner: "Other business owners have told me that Lee Green used to be a good place for parents to meet up and chat while they did their shopping. Now it is just a dead environment and we are definitely suffering".

It may be true that, at the time of this survey, Lee Green's Leegate Shopping Centre was due to close for redevelopment. Yet, the huge Sainsburys that clutches at Lee Green's heart will continue to ensure that small, independent shops never prosper. This supermarket has created a shopping desert beyond its check-outs.

The combination of well-stocked supermarkets, home fridges and freezers should mean that today's families enjoy a more varied diet than in the 1950s – with all that implies for improved health. Sadly, the exact opposite is true. Most people fill their fridges and freezers with junk food, unhealthy snacks and packs of beer. A diet of manufactured convenience foods and alcohol, combined with lack of exercise, has produced a 21st-century population in declining health.

---oOo---

- 7 -

"Something" of a Sweet Tooth

Sweet rationing ended in Britain in 1953. Surprisingly, perhaps, toffee apples became the biggest seller as restrictions were lifted. In the late 1950s toffee apples remained popular. There were the usual brown toffee apples and the latest thing – apples covered in a bright red, toffee-like hard crust. It was a great way to loosen milk teeth, but I had passed that stage.

Aunty Ivy, my mother's elder sister, lived with us at 48 Hedgley Street. She took a shine to me from the first. It was her weekly practice to buy sweets for the kids. Every evening she would invite my brother and I to "choose something". At the age of six I regarded "something" as a generic term for sweets.

My choice usually involved a chocolate bar. The various brands all had their distinctive merits. Cadbury's, Fry's and Nestlé's received my attention as often as possible. Nestlé's rhymed with "settles" in those days.

My Aunt is largely responsible for my deep love of Cadbury's *Dairy Milk*. This passion is undiminished by time and exposure to more exotic Continental alternatives. *Dairy Milk* was launched in 1905. Initially, it came in large blocks, to be broken into penny bars at the counter. Consumption of *Dairy Milk* should be limited, but this requires willpower beyond the reach of most mortals. The long British love affair with this chocolate has been reinforced by some memorable promotional campaigns, many based on self-reward (including the award of a "CDM", on completion of the chores). I remember the 1950s penny bars – so small that today's kids would polish them off in one mouthful. I could suck a penny bar until its end began to flop over. Cadbury's *Fruit & Nut* and *Wholenut* were much loved but catered for adult tastes.

Dairy Milk was a firm favourite when choosing "something". Nevertheless, my hand would sometimes hover over a bar of *Aero*. Plain, white, orange, peppermint and various other trendy varieties have been made, but the original 1950s *Rowntrees Aero* was a milk chocolate masterpiece. The bubbly manufacturing process had been patented in 1935 (one of the very few good things to come from that decade). Some 6,000 tonnes of *Aero* was sold in the first year. It was relaunched in 1950 after an absence of nine years due to the war.

My Aunt was quick to learn. Only the most popular "somethings" were stockpiled, including Fry's chocolate. Fry's was the pinnacle of perfection. *Five Boys* chocolate was a delight, its wrapper portraying those truculent little rascals (reading, from left to right: "Desperation, Pacification, Expectation, Acclamation, Realisation" – the latter appearing as a child in ecstasy). How clever of my Aunt to invent the daily "something" ritual, which evoked all five emotions! Naturally, as a six-year-old I had no knowledge of the 1902 Fry's advertisement which declared: "Five girls want Five Boys and will have no other". A 21st-century Creative Director would have to be both brave and foolish to put such a message forward for a campaign.

Fry's *Sandwich* bars, a marriage of milk and plain chocolate, were another delight. Less successful Fry's products (at least to my taste) included *Turkish Delight*. This bar might have been "full of Eastern promise" but it was too sweet for my taste. *Turkish Delight* has a loyal following, no doubt attracted by the "harem girl" TV commercials. This product has stayed the course – it was first introduced in 1914.

Something about Fry's chocolate made it especially delicious. Joseph Fry began production in 1759. He applied the latest technology available – James Watt's steam engine – to grind cocoa beans. In 1822 the company became J.S. Fry & Sons, Britain's leading chocolate manufacturer. Twenty-five years later Fry's made the first chocolate bar suitable for mass consumption. In 1873 it made Britain's first chocolate Easter egg.

We always had our chocolate eggs on Easter Sunday. We had to wait until after breakfast – Mum and Dad thought that boiled eggs and "soldiers" should come first. We usually had five or six Easter Eggs, with one or two containing chocolates (usually *Cadbury's Milk Tray* and *Smarties*). It was my habit to eat one egg immediately, then break up the rest into bite-sized pieces. I carried them around in a paper bag and ate a piece whenever I felt like it.

---oOo---

My personal favourites at the sweet shop included *Crunchy*. I melted away the "honeycomb" with the tip of my tongue (until it became too sore to continue). I also enjoyed a four-finger *Kit-Kat,* costing a "tanner". "Have a break – have a Kit-Kat!" was coined in the 1950s. *Kit-Kat*, along with *Aero*, celebrated its 75th birthday in 2010. According to Nestlé, 150 *Kit-Kats* are consumed every second around the world. I bought mine from the sweet shop in Manor Lane, situated near the "Lollipop" traffic crossing leading to Lee Manor School's gate. I never spent money on *Mars Bars*. I found its filling too sticky and sweet (although I liked the thick chocolate and caramel layer). The claim that "A Mars a day helps you work, rest and play" came later, in the 1960s.

Sweet heaven: the newsagents where the author bought most of his sweets, as it is today. It is only two minutes from the gate of Lee Manor School. There is still a barbers next door. The author had his first haircut here, at the age of six months. A child's haircut cost 2/6 (12.5p).

I never liked white chocolate. The "Milky Bar Kid", who came along in 1961, made little impression on me. I also disliked *Penguins*, much preferring *Bandit* chocolate wafers. *Wagon Wheels* also made little impact. How could anything that looked that good be such a disappointment? The *Wagon Wheels'* size appealed to childish greed. It was huge! These large, circular biscuits were topped with marshmallow and had a chocolate-flavoured coating. *Wagon Wheels* were launched at the 1948 Olympia Food Fair. Size, apparently, *is* everything when it comes to *Wagon Wheels*. The manufacturers deny claims that today's *Wagon Wheels* are smaller. Apparently, the UK *Wagon Wheel* is little changed, but it is 14 mm smaller than its Australian counterpart (although a British *Wagon Wheel* is 4 mm thicker). So there!

---oOo---

Small sweets were sold by the quarter, two ounces or "four for a penny". I usually ignored *Blackjacks, Fruit Salad Chews, Sherbet Lemons* and *Raspberry Drops* but I liked toffee. Mackintosh's *Toffo* tasted wonderful – especially when warm and soft (it paid to keep them in your pocket). John Mackintosh was smart. When he opened his shop in Halifax, Yorkshire, during 1890, he declared that his toffee would be "not too hard, not too soft". He was entirely successful in getting the balance right.

I loved *Penny Arrow* toffee bars, but remember my enthusiasm more than the product. Other popular toffee brands included *Blue Bird, Liquorice Rolls* and Callard & Bowser *Creamline*. Given my preferences, chocolate-covered *Rolos* were an ideal sweet. There is that disturbing question, first posed in the 1980s: "Do you love anyone enough to give them your last Rolo?" I would not have coped with such an awful challenge in the 1950s.

As for winter sweets, I liked *Cough Candy Twist* and *Barley Sugar* was acceptable, but I disliked *Humbugs, Bullseyes* and *Aniseed Balls*. I saw no point in *Gobstoppers*; they lasted forever yet failed to entertain. *Jelly Babies* were (are) delicious, especially the black ones. When introduced in 1918 they were known as *Peace Babies*. This name became something of an embarrassment in 1939. Production stopped in wartime, then resumed (the original name being appropriate once again). Nevertheless, *Peace Babies* became *Jelly Babies* in 1953. Perhaps the hostile attitude of the Russians had something to do with that.

Milk Gums, or *Milk Bottles*, were nondescript, as were *Fizzy Cola Gums*, but *Victory V* lozenges had a pungent, addictive taste. They probably had more punch in their original guise (the ingredients once included chloroform).

Some 1950s sweets were bizarre, at least to modern tastes and the rigours of political correctness. Liquorice *Smoker's Sets* were popular, complete with sweet cigarettes, tobacco and liquorice pipes. Sweet cigarettes were thin tubes of white candy with a red end – representing the glowing tip. They came in replica cigarette packets free of health warnings. What would today's evangelical anti-smoking lobby make of that? Paper-wrapped *Chocolate Cigarettes* were also available. Today, *Sweet Cigarettes* are sold in parts of the world where political correctness is a tender plant, rather than a *Triffid*.

With my pocket money almost spent, the last penny could buy a couple of *Shrimps*, candy sweets which disappeared rapidly upon contact with saliva. I was not over-fond of *Sherbet*, but bought it occasionally. I remember sharing a *Sherbet Fountain* with Karen Green, my 10-year-old girlfriend of the time.

This romantic tryst took place outside a red telephone box on the corner of Handen Road and Manor Lane.

Everyone tried to like *Flying Saucers* – sickly, UFO-shaped rice paper sweets filled with *Sherbet*. Stranger still were the *Jamboree Bag* and the misdescribed *Lucky Bag*. Both were famed for disappointing kids, containing only a handful of poor quality sweets and one or two small plastic toys.

Returning to matters of the heart, it was always possible to make overtures to a cute, pig-tailed girl by offering a *Love Heart*. This was a rather sour-tasting fizzy sweet inscribed with short "love" messages, presented within a heart-shaped outline.

I was never enthusiastic about mints and happily ignored *Refreshers*, a rather gritty fruit-flavoured fizzy sweet. *Polo Mints* and *Murray Mints* were acceptable, but lacked purpose. In contrast, chewing gum and bubble gum were popular. My favourite chewing gum was *YZ*; it had an owl on a small square packet containing a few lozenges in foil. *YZ* was dispensed from a machine giving free gum at every fourth go (when the knob's curved arrow faced forwards). *Wrigley's Spearmint*, *Double Mint* and *Juicy Fruit* were popular, as were various makes of bubble gum. *Bazooka* was a leading brand, its packaging featuring "Bazooka Joe". Brooklyn-based Topps Company introduced this product after World War Two (when *Bazooka* meant something quite different from bubble gum).

---oOo---

It was a pleasure to confirm the marketing message for *Treets*: "The milk chocolate that melts in your mouth, not in your hands". *Smarties* were yummy yet failed to deliver sufficient chocolate. *Smarties* is an old confectionery brand; the product was first introduced in 1882 as *Chocolate Beans* and became *Smarties* in 1937. They came in red, orange, green, yellow, pink, violet and brown (the latter later replaced by blue). *Smarties* always make me think of a very successful 1960s advertising jingle: "Buy some for Lulu."

Rowntree's Fruit Gums could be made to last. In an interesting reflection on social norms, the 1956 message "Don't forget the fruit gums, Mum!" was thought to be too pushy. It became "Don't forget the fruit gums, chum!" I enjoyed making the knobbly bits on a fruit gum disappear. Blackcurrant was the clear favourite, followed by red. I found fruit gums in boxes more delicious. Sadly, I had few opportunities to confirm this preference, as a box of fruit gums was quite expensive, at one shilling (5p). *Rowntree's Pastilles* also scored highly, with purple the clear frontrunner.

Most people of my vintage seem to recall *Spangles* with great affection, but I found these boiled sweets – square-shaped with a dimple on each face – rather boring. The *Old English Spangles* variety was loathsome. *Spangles*, first introduced in the 1950s, were withdrawn in the 1980s (but with a brief revival in 1994).

---ooo---

"Stop me and buy one!" must be one of the most familiar of advertising slogans. Between the wars and into the early 1950s, ice cream salesmen on bikes (tricycles) were a common sight at the seaside and in parks. In the 1930s they included my father, with his Wall's bike. Things changed when the ice cream van arrived. Ice cream was big business in the 1950s; there were some 20,000 van owners, or "mobilisers". The ice cream van's loud chimes provided the soundtrack to our childhood. Popular tunes included *Greensleeves*, *Yankee Doodle* and *Oranges and Lemons*. Some vans sold delicious soft ice cream, topped with a "99" chocolate flake. This was the most popular sale from vans.

Ice cream as we know it originated in 17th-century Italy. Ice cream in 1950s Britain consisted of a cone (or "cornet"), a "brick" (a slab of ice cream between two rectangular wafers), a tub or a lolly (usually frozen fruit squash). The Lyon's Maid *Orange Maid*, introduced in 1954 and the first lolly of any quality, was made with real orange juice. It was known as "The drink on a stick". The *Mivvi* followed – a strawberry lolly with Cornish ice cream inside. I quite liked its sister product, the pineapple *Mivvi*. Vanilla was the dominant ice cream flavour, but there was also "Neapolitan" (layered vanilla, strawberry and chocolate).

---ooo---

My favourite fizzy drink, *Tizer*, was bright red and came in glass bottles with a screw stopper. "Tizer the Appetiser" was launched in 1924 by the man also responsible for *Irn-Bru*. R. White's, a leading lemonade brand in the 1950s, became even bigger in the 1970s thanks to a much-imitated TV commercial, "I'm a secret lemonade drinker" (featuring Elvis Costello's dad). I liked *Cream Soda*, devised in America over a century earlier. This sweet fizzy drink is flavoured with vanilla (a substance offering proof positive of the existence of Heaven).

Coca Cola, in its unmistakable bottle, was a big treat. *Pepsi* was an alternative with a stronger "bite", at least to my palate. *Pepsi* bubbles always went up my nose. At that time, of course, the ring-pull was a long way off (invented in the early 1960s, it first appeared in Britain in 1970).

The "fizz" in fizzy drinks is attributed to Joseph Schweppe of Switzerland, who introduced carbonated mineral water in the 1780s. Its manufacture was not without hazard; corks were hammered in and tied with copper wire. Workers wore gloves and face shields, as the bottles often exploded!

R. White's competitors included Corona ("It's got a sparkle in the middle and a tingle at the top!"). In the 1890s William Evans built a mineral water plant producing ginger beer, lemonade, orangeade, raspberryade and dandelion and burdock. Business boomed. In the 1920s the Welsh Hills Soft Drinks Company became Corona, with a distribution network throughout England and Wales.

In 1940 large fleets of soft drinks delivery lorries were requisitioned by the military for war service. Production became difficult during the war years, but the industry made a strong recovery when peace came. Corona was eventually taken over by the Beecham Group.

Other 1950s soft drinks, such as *Idris,* bring back fond memories. Thomas Williams had a factory in Camden Town, London – the Victorian home of the Idris Table Water Company. I remember *Idris* for its hypnotic 1950s jingle: "I drink Idris, I drink Idris, Idris when I's dri". My favourite orange drink, however, was *Kia-Ora* (apparently, a Maori saying: "Good luck"). Kia-Ora was launched in Britain in 1917. *Kia-Ora Suncrush* had a distinct and delicious taste. It also had a catchy 1950s slogan: "We all adora Kia-Ora!"

The ultimate 1950s orange drink, however, was the *Jubbly* or, to be more precise, the *Frozen Jubbly*. This was 4d worth of heaven. Firstly, it was huge. Secondly, it was a peculiar shape; it came in an ingenious waxed tetrahedron. The phrase "Lovely Jubbly" was immortalised by *Only Fools and Horses'* "Del Boy". This slogan is a rare example of advertising telling the *absolute truth*. A *Frozen Jubbly* was LOVELY. The treat began by tearing off a corner, sucking out the orange and leaving a patch of colourless ice. The next stage was to bash it against a wall and suck out the recharged orange slush. A *Jubbly* lasted forever and turned the consumer's lips and tongue bright orange. Lovely Jubbly!

---oOo---

When Mum had a birthday I scraped together enough money to buy her a small box of chocolates. One possibility was *Cadbury's Milk Tray*. There were also *Maltesers* – "chocolates with the less fattening centres" (a claim dependent on just how many *Maltesers* were consumed). Mum's favourite was *Black Magic*. Sales in the 1950s were backed by some amazing hyperbole: "Nothing sweetens the atmosphere so quickly as a box of Black Magic chocolates. There's a certain something about those centres that's irresistible; so many, so marvellous: liquid cherry for brightening her eyes, Montelimar for parting her lips, orange creme to make her heart beat faster..." Had I known what I was doing, I would never have brought such a dangerous treat into an otherwise peaceful household! In any event, when offered the box, I found these chocolates uninteresting, with the exception of the cherry, caramel and Brazil (the three everyone else liked).

---ooo---

There has been a slow-motion nuclear explosion in consumer choice over the past 50 years. Successful products are now copied, repackaged and endlessly reconfigured. Yet many leading brands of the 1950s still prosper, including *Dairy Milk*, *Aero*, *Kit-Kat* and *Mars*.

Manufacturers struggle to hoodwink 21st-century consumers. Nevertheless, many chocolate bars have shrunk yet sell for the same price. It was big news when a £1 bar of *Dairy Milk* lost two chunks. While some chocolate bars have shrunk, others have grown (the product being sold in larger or even double size bars). Curiously, all price movements favour the manufacturer, rather than the chocolate-lover. Cadbury's shrank from 140 g to 120 g. The *Toblerone* 200 g bar declined to 170 g (one less "mountain peak" to swallow). *Mars* was trimmed from 62.5 g to 58 g (so providing less energy to "work, rest and play"). A 140 g bag of *Maltesers* became a 120 g bag, holding nine fewer sweets (presumably, in line with the "less fattening" principle). As for *Rolos*, they now have 10 sweets rather than 11 (so enhancing the traditionally high value placed on "the last Rolo").

Manufacturers have struggled to defend their margins as cocoa prices soar. Recent years have seen substantial changes in the industry's ownership structures. Fry's merged with Cadbury very early on – in 1919 – but the Fry's name survived until 1981. More recently, there was public hostility when Cadbury was taken over by the American giant Kraft. Rowntree acquired Mackintosh in 1969 but was taken over, in turn, by Nestlé in 1988. Three years earlier, Rowntree sold

Kit-Kat, *Smarties* and *Aero* to Nestlé. *Aero* remains popular. In Japan, exotic *Aero* flavours include "Vanilla Milkshake" and "Green Tea".

Today's sweet manufacturers have curious ideas. *Smarties*, for example, are produced in tubes, mini cartons and "sharing bags". The idea of sharing *Smarties* would be alien to most children. Today, I love *Wispa* and *Twirl*. The advent of bite-sized treat bags of these sweets is, to my mind, a rare compensation for the modern world. Sharing, of course, is out of the question.

Since the 1950s the world of ice cream has been turned upside down by market forces and changing consumer behaviour. The national fleet of ice cream vans has shrunk by around 80 per cent. The trade was crippled by the advent of domestic freezers and supermarket multipacks. Surviving van owners now wrestle with soaring vehicle costs, sky-high insurance premiums, costly Street Trader's Licences and pettifogging bans on sales at locations near schools. The van owners now work all year round; years ago, they could afford to take the winter off. Yet, some things are unchanged – Vanilla remains the most popular ice cream flavour.

As for fizzy drinks, *Tizer* has been sold in purple and green variants and there was a short-lived flirtation with "real fruit juice". *Tizer* marketing has been of mixed quality. One campaign showed kids with their faces pressed against a glass surface, with the message "How many kids can you get in your fridge?" This failed to impress the Royal Society for the Prevention of Accidents, given the deaths of small children trapped in refrigerators.

It seems fitting to conclude on a romantic note. In February 2012 the daughter of two celebrities arrived for "London Fashion Week" wearing an unusual dress. It was covered in a design mimicking *Love Hearts*, but with sentiments rather different from those of the 1950s. The original sweets had harmless messages, such as "I love you", "Tease me" and, most shocking of all, "Wicked". Examples on this dress, however, included: "Blow me", "Choke", "Drink Poison", and "Please Drown". Romance is not what it was!

---ooo---

– 8 –

Toys for Boys

My earliest memory is of playing on the floor. We had a new carpet in the front room. Mum towered over me, busy at the ironing board. The iron was plugged into the light socket. She was pressing a shirt and I was loading my friction motor toy milk float with fluff from the new carpet. I was three years old.

It was soon time for bed and I was tucked up with my favourite cuddly toy, a pink rabbit with ultra long floppy ears. This rabbit stayed with the family for many years. By the time it had lost its appeal to my sister, the only way to discover its original marshmallow pink colour was to lift up its ears, where tiny areas had been protected from the effects of age and grubby hands.

In the 1950s, new toys came only at Christmas and birthdays. I don't remember much about my birthdays, other than the teaparties when I was very small. We had triangular sandwiches with the crusts cut off. There was a small birthday cake with candles to be blown out. We also had fancy cakes, topped with a small iced biscuit, jelly and ice cream and *Cadbury's Chocolate Fingers* washed down with orange squash or *Ribena*.

A birthday card from Aunty Ivy: cherubic faces from a 1950s illustrator.

Christmas was always more exciting, due to the lengthy build-up of anticipation. It began at school. We made endless paper chains with small strips of coloured paper with a sticky edge, which were looped together. The glue built-up on my tongue after a while. We were also shown how to make "Shepherds' Lanterns" from thick paper, which were painted and then borne home in triumph. There were also annual visits to Father Christmas at Chiesmans Store in Lewisham.

Santa's expression sets the tone at Chiesman's store, Lewisham, in November 1952. We had no idea that Father Christmas, in reality, was known to our father as Bert Smith, Southern Railway Foreman at Hither Green Station.

At home, Dad bought a small Christmas Tree, which was placed in a bucket. This was filled with earth, to keep it stable, then covered in red crepe paper. We had a small string of fairy lights and a large cardboard box full of glass balls, tinsel and plastic decorations. We enjoyed helping to decorate the tree and were careful to place the small, foil-wrapped chocolate Santas within easy reach. The tree looked wonderful but Mum knew that it would soon begin to drop its needles over the carpet.

Mum had made a Christmas Pudding and Dad produced a turkey. On one occasion he arrived with a fresh bird, placed it on the kitchen table and began to draw it. The sight and smell were revolting. I decided that I would concentrate on the roast potatoes and gravy. Christmas dinner was the only meal, beyond breakfast, that Dad cooked during the year. The ritual began when he persuaded Mum to pull a Christmas Cracker. He then donned the paper hat, went to the Bureau cupboard and brought out the *Gordons*. He poured himself a glass of neat gin and turned his attentions to the turkey. The meal was ready around three hours later. By that time, he would have polished off his second glass of gin – the only spirits he consumed during the year.

It was difficult for the kids to go to sleep on Christmas Eve. We had no stockings at the bottom of our beds; stockings were too small! Pillowcases were Santa's favoured means of delivery. Eventually we went to sleep and woke early to find those heavily pregnant pillowcases. Later, when I began to have my suspicions about Santa, I made a real effort to catch Mum and Dad in the act of present-giving, but sleep got the better of me and I never succeeded. There were no regrets in the thrill of stumbling out of bed and diving into my pillowcase.

One Christmas Colin and I received battery-powered lanterns amongst our presents. These were ideal for setting up camp on the stairs. I turned the lights out and settled into the upper landing. I could fire down on Colin, illuminated in the red glow from his lantern.

Christmas Day was a time when the answer to almost any request was "yes". "Can I have a tangerine?" "Yes!" "Can I have the purple *Quality Street* sweet?" "Yes!" It was a day of delights and Boxing Day always seemed a bit of an anti-climax.

---ooo---

I have no memory of where I kept my toys; they were probably stowed under the bed. I certainly found room for my magnificent model garage, a present from Aunty Ivy. This had a futuristic design, the building having rounded profiles. I spent a lot of time on the carpet, putting cars in the garage and making loud, engine-like noises.

My most treasured possession was parked in a corner of the scullery. This was my *Triang* tricycle, finished in bright red. Its cavernous boot was just right for storing pink rabbits and other essentials. I was allowed to pedal my trike along the pavement, but with orders not to go more than four or five doors down.

Manor Lane Infants School had a good stock of toys. I liked the sand pit and the powder paints. I enjoyed mixing the paint more than the painting. Another favourite was a play set of wooden blocks and pegs. It was easy to construct huge battleships. I was fascinated by the *Bayko* construction set, with its bricks, roof tiles, windows and the thin steel rods holding everything together. We used up plenty of energy during lessons, games and in the playground. The afternoon break was great. We were told to fold our arms, lean forward onto our desks and snooze. What a wonderful school!

Kids played with yo-yos and hula hoops. I had a bright red and yellow yo-yo but never got it to do much. Hula hoops (the 1950s incarnation of a toy that is thousands of years old) were for girls. They became a national fad in 1959. The *Barbie* doll was launched that year at a New York City toy fair. *Barbie* was another instant hit with the girls.

Dad and I preferred to spend our Saturday mornings making lead soldiers. He would bring out the pot, drop in pieces of scrap lead and heat it up over a burner. When it was bubbling nicely, he would pour the molten lead into moulds, producing toy infantrymen of the Great War period. When I got fed up with them, they were returned to the pot, to reappear in a new guise. I suppose this Saturday morning habit broke just about every health and safety rule going (although lead, at that time, was not seen as especially hazardous). I had my nose close to the pot, watching the lead melt and bubble. Nevertheless, I still passed my 11-Plus (although I should confess that I have done some stupid things in my time!).

Virtually every small boy in the 1950s had a "cowboy outfit": a hat, a fancy waistcoat with fringes at the pockets and "leggings". Around my waist I wore a belt and holster for my "six-gun", a cap-firing revolver. I also had a toy *Winchester* repeating rifle, just in case the six-gun was shot out of my hand. Sadly, our small suburban back garden had no room for a horse. Some kids dressed up as Indians, but most wanted to be cowboys. Yet, I did have a very nice bow and a set of arrows fitted with suckers. Rubber suckers apart, an arrow in the eye could have had serious consequences. Fortunately, my brother and I escaped injury – although we were often scolded for licking the suckers and firing arrows at the windows. They would stick and quiver on the glass, making a satisfying thud that frightened Mum.

Cowboy outfits were donned when playing in the garden or indoors. My favourite position was on the stairs, firing down at my brother and filling the hall with the acrid stink of caps. Caps were great. When I held that small, round box of caps in my hand, I really felt I could blow up something! When bored with shooting my brother, I would set up my clockwork train, with its green painted locomotive and two carriages. It took about six seconds to complete a lap of the small, circular track. I put obstacles in the way, to cause derailments and make things more interesting.

---OOO---

Happy days: the author looks content in his cowboy outfit but brother Colin seems despondent – probably because he has been shot so many times by the cap gun. Keeping us in order is a friend, Sandra. Nell, the family's black and tan mongrel, is just in the picture.

A relative (I don't recall who) bought me an amazing book, full of card press-out models of the most advanced aircraft of the time, including the delta-winged Avro Vulcan bomber. Unfortunately, the instructions for assembly were virtually impossible to comprehend. It was certainly well beyond the capabilities of a seven-year-old. I suspect it might also have been beyond my Dad, who never attempted to put one together. So, the book sat in a drawer and gathered dust. It is a pity it didn't survive; I imagine it would be a collector's item today.

There were other disappointments. Another relative promised me a steam engine and I expected nothing less than the *Flying Scotsman*! My face must have been a picture when he handed me a small green metal plate mounting a tiny piston, wheel and boiler. Dad thought it was great and soon got it going with a teaspoon of methylated spirit. I was not impressed. I preferred straightforward things, such as *Mr Potato Head*. I tried to produce the ugliest possible face, putting ears where the eyes should have been and further disfiguring the spud by putting the nose on upside down.

The family's long tin bath, filled in the scullery every Friday evening, was perfect for speed trials with another prize: my clockwork Air Sea Rescue launch. This wonderful model boat came complete with RAF roundels and brass propeller and rudder.

Some ambitions stayed out of reach. I had a basic *Meccano* set but building a working model of Tower Bridge was beyond my abilities. I lacked the practical skills necessary to make a box cart, but had a friend who owned an example equipped with large pram wheels and rope steering. One afternoon we took off down a steep hill that funnelled into a narrow, walled alley. We touched the wall, turned over and my leg lost the skin over a six-inch long deep graze filled with gravel. That wound took a long time to heal.

Putting this upset behind me, I turned to sedentary pursuits. The family occasionally played board games, usually *Monopoly*. I was happier messing about with my microscope. I pricked my finger and studied blood smeared on a glass slide. I pulled the wings off dead flies and studied them under the microscope. I experimented with my chemistry set. I grew large, deep blue copper sulphate crystals. I used substances like Isinglass and potassium permanganate, but I can't remember for what purpose. I made every effort to produce the most terrible smells. My chemistry set was amazing: if I had tried harder, I might have blown up the scullery. Looking back, Mum and Dad were incredibly tolerant. Perhaps they considered the risks worthwhile, if this was my first tentative step towards a Nobel Prize.

When 10 years old I was given a modest *Hornby* electric train set, bought secondhand. I had two engines – an express and a small tank engine – together with carriages, track and a small, black transformer. I found it all rather boring and eventually got rid of it. This was the first time I had sold anything. It went to the owner of the local fish and chip shop, who wanted it for his son.

On reaching 11 my main interest (beyond playing football in the park) was an impressive collection of *Airfix* model aircraft. I had the patience to put together these plastic model kits, following the instructions and diagrams. Unfortunately, I always managed to get the glue, or "plastic cement", all over my fingers. I painted the models, using small tins of *Humbrol* enamel paint. When assembled and painted, the aircraft were suspended from my bedroom ceiling by thick thread. Mum hated these "dust harbourers".

It took a while to get my hands on an *Airfix* Lancaster, priced at 7/6 (seven shillings and sixpence, or 37.5p). One of my relations came to stay. He was doing his National Service in the RAF. He told Mum he wanted to buy me the Lancaster model kit. She said it was too expensive and, to my horror, he promptly agreed! I had to wait until my next birthday to build this four-engined bomber.

Something profound happened at the age of 10. My parents bought me the *Odhams Encyclopaedia for Children*. I had my head in this book every evening, reading about dinosaurs, the invention of the diesel engine, the splitting of the atom and X-rays. The book's introduction declared: "This is an encyclopaedia, a sort of Aladdin's Cave stuffed, not with jewels, but with facts, more marvellous than jewels and often no less precious". I agreed! Mum and Dad took note and went on to purchase *The Book of Knowledge* – a set of eight hefty volumes requiring rather more commitment on my part. I set to work on them. After a few months I could pick any volume and anticipate what I would find in a given chapter. I also developed an irritating habit – asking people if they were aware that light travelled at 186,000 miles per second or that the sun was 93 million miles from Earth. I had yet to learn that most people are uninterested in such trivia, especially when eating Sunday lunch!

For light relief I collected humorous bubble gum cards illustrated by Jack Davis, the iconic American artist who contributed to *MAD* magazine. Their messages still make me laugh: "Your teeth are like stars... they come out at night!" "You ought to be on the stage... there's one leaving in 10 minutes!" "Your face is like a million dollars... green and wrinkled!"

Meccano Ltd took over *Bayko* and continued to make the construction sets until 1967. Today, there are mature *Bayko* enthusiasts all over the world. Some make *Bayko* supermodels – airports, skyscrapers and so on. Some even cast their own components, to extend the creative possibilities! The standard sets are often available on ebay. I wonder what happened to my set? Perhaps someone is bidding for it, right now? Please note that I would like it returned, together with my Air Sea Rescue launch!

---oOo---

- 9 -

Top of the Pops

Pop charts were new in the 1950s. The "Hit Parade" was introduced by *New Musical Express* in 1952. Previously, "hits" were judged on sheet music sales. In contrast, the *NME* chart of 14 November, 1952, was based on record sales at a representative sample of 20 stores. Being just three years old at the time, I was blissfully unaware of the first "No.1", Al Martino's *Here is my Heart*. It topped the chart for nine weeks.

Three performers – Frankie Laine, Guy Mitchell and Elvis Presley – had four No.1s each during the 1950s. The rise of Rock and Roll was underpinned by two songs: Bill Haley and his Comets' *Rock Around the Clock* and Elvis Presley's *Jailhouse Rock*. *Rock Around the Clock* might have been the biggest selling single of the 1950s but Bill Haley's kiss curl did nothing for me. Elvis was different, with that harder edge to *Jailhouse Rock* and the amazing *Heartbreak Hotel*.

The 1950s charts were rich in variety. The chart-toppers of 1953 included Guy Mitchell's *She Wears Red Feathers*, Frankie Laine's *I Believe* and Lita Roza's *How Much is that Doggy in the Window?* Generally, the top slot was dominated by ballads and "easy listening". The 1956 Hit Parade included Ronnie Hilton's *No Other Love*, Doris Day's *Que Sera, Sera* and the distinctly 1940s sound of Anne Shelton's *Lay Down Your Arms* (although, perhaps, this was a clever choice for release in the year of the Suez Crisis).

Things changed in 1957, when Elvis Presley's appropriately-titled *All Shook Up* was released. This was also the year of Lonnie Donegan's *Cumberland Gap*, Paul Anka's *Diana* and The Crickets' *That'll Be The Day*. The new music snowballed into 1958 and 1959, with Jerry Lee Lewis' *Great Balls of Fire*, Connie Francis' *Stupid Cupid*, the Everly Brothers' *Claudette* and *All I Have to do is Dream*, Buddy Holly's *It Doesn't Matter Anymore* and Bobby Darin's *Dream Lover*. There were also big hits from new British stars, including Adam Faith's *What Do You Want?* and Cliff Richard's *Living Doll* and *Travelling Light*.

---oOo---

Television opened the pop floodgates, with shows such as *Juke Box Jury*, Six-*Five Special* and *Oh Boy!* The BBC's *Six-Five Special* was broadcast live at five past six on Saturday evenings. It filled a slot formerly occupied by *Toddlers' Truce* – the TV close-down allowing parents to put the kids to bed.

Six-Five Special was not alone. Associated Rediffusion began broadcasting *Cool for Cats* in late 1956. This 15-minute show played records, with Kent Walton providing commentary. The programme, decorated by the Dougie Squires Dancers, soldiered on until 1959.

Six-Five Special was hosted by Pete Murray, Jim Dale, Josephine Douglas and, rather strangely, the boxer Freddie Mills. Don Lang and his Frantic Five were resident. The programme, with its steam train theme (The Six-Five Special's coming down the line... the Six-Five Special's right on time), was first broadcast on 16 February, 1957. It was to run for six weeks but lasted into the following year. The producers were Jack Good and Josephine Douglas and the regulars included Marty Wilde (Reginald Smith), Tommy Steele (Thomas Hicks), Petula Clark, Terry Dene and Lonnie Donegan. There were also guest appearances from Bernie Winters and Spike Milligan. Jack Good took exception to a BBC policy which sought to dilute the music with educational interludes and public information. He joined ABC and made the all-music show *Oh Boy!* This crushed *Six-Five Special*, which was dropped – with some relief – by an unenthusiastic BBC. Yet, it then made an attempt to take the high ground with *Dig This* and *Drumbeat* (both have been deleted from my memory banks).

Young audiences wanted music rather than chat. Anyone watching *Six-Five Special* today would be struck by its self-conscious, patronising style. Yet the fact is that these shows were RADICAL. When first broadcast, *Six-Five Special* felt like it came from another planet – *Planet Fun*. To the more conservative, this planet was populated by razor-wielding Teddy Boys and young girls prone to orgasmic fits of screaming.

Oh Boy!, occupying the 6 pm slot in direct competition with *Six-Five Special*, was broadcast live from the Hackney Empire. It was graced by the presence of Lord Rockingham's Xl, with the Vernons Girls adding essential glamour. Later, in September 1959, *Oh Boy!* was succeeded by *Boy Meets Girls*, another Jack Good show.

These programmes were an odd mix of Rock and Roll, jazz and skiffle, seasoned with lame jokes and trite comments. It was very contrived and often boring, but a live show like *Oh Boy!* could never be taken for granted. There were gripping performances from big names, including a sinister-looking Gene Vincent and the great Eddie Cochran. Cliff Richard (Harry Webb) and The Drifters (later, The Shadows) were regulars. They were huge following the October 1958 hit *Move it*. Cliff appeared on 20 *Oh Boy!* shows; other guests included Billy Fury and Brenda Lee (Little Miss Dynamite).

When *Drumbeat* finished in 1959, it was succeeded by DJ David Jacobs' *Juke Box Jury*. The Jury's show business celebrities included Thora Hird, Jayne Mansfield, Alfred Hitchcock and Zsa Zsa Gabor. *Juke Box Jury* had a catchy theme, which was a big hit in its own right. First broadcast on 1 June, 1959, the programme ran in its original format until December 1967. It attracted a Saturday night audience of 12 million in 1962. New releases were reviewed and "misses" declared by a loud hooter. Another feature was the surprise guest. The performer would appear after the Jury had given its verdict. This show had something for everyone: teenagers wanted the music and parents enjoyed agreeing with the acerbic comments of more mature jurors. The most famous episode was broadcast on 7 December, 1963, when the jurors were The Beatles. It was watched by 23 million people. On 4 July, 1964, the jury increased to five, to accommodate The Rolling Stones.

---ooo---

This wave of pop music broke around me but had little direct impact on our 1950s home. I was stuck with a wind-up portable playing 78s. We had a collection of ancient records, including what I knew as the "German hiking song" – the Oberkirchen Children's Choir singing *The happy wanderer*. This was written just after World War Two, at a time when many Europeans felt that the Germans were too fond of "wandering". This song had an unforgettable chorus:

> *"Val-deri, val-dera,*
> *Val-deri*
> *Val-dera-ha-ha-ha-ha-ha*
> *Val-deri, val-dera*
> *My knapsack on my back."*

This was a world apart from the pop revolution unfolding just a few minutes from my home. A Lee Green shop sold Dansette record-players and the latest 45 rpm records. The Dansette soon became a household essential and its manufacturers struggled to keep pace with demand. These record-players were finished in "Leatherette", in shades of blue, green, red and pink. The main feature was the "autochanger", which allowed stacks of 45s to be played. The Redding family's example was in blue and cream.

Records were expensive and I had to choose with great care. My first 45 was *Apache*, by The Shadows. I played it so many times that I became part Apache. This was No. 1 for five weeks in 1960. It was from the pen of singer/songwriter Jerry Lordan, who also wrote *Wonderful Land* – another massive hit for The Shadows. *Apache* was a sensation; it created the definitive sound for The Shadows and those who sought to emulate them.

The Shadows had around 70 chart hits, half as The Shadows and the rest with Cliff Richard. Founder members were lead guitarist Hank Marvin, rhythm guitarist Bruce Welch, bass player Terence "Jet" Harris (who thought up The Shadows name) and drummer Tony Meehan. Marvin and Welch had played together in a school skiffle band. Harris and Meehan went on to enjoy chart success in their own right.

For those unfamiliar with The Shadows' sound, I recommend their flawless recording of *The Stranger*, followed immediately by the iconic *FBI*. *Mustang* is also very good. This group demonstrated the importance of having a distinctive, unmistakable sound. The Shadows' sound was based on American Fender guitars, British Vox amplifiers and echo units.

Fame imposed stresses. Tony Meehan left The Shadows in 1961, to be replaced by Brian Bennett. Harris was succeeded in April 1962 by Brian "Licorice" Locking. My memories focus on the original line-up and the remarkable music produced in a few short years. Today, The Shadows remain the most popular instrumental group in British musical history.

American singer Del Shannon recorded my second 45, *Runaway*. Released in February 1961, it soon reached No. 1. Other hits followed for Shannon but *Runaway* was special. I played this so much that it penetrated my soul. I seemed to hear it everywhere I went. Over 50 years later, I still love *Runaway*. I was thrilled to hear it again, in a reworked version by Del Shannon, as the theme for the TV series *Crime Story*.

The year 1961 also saw a remarkable hit from singer and actor John Leyton. *Johnny, remember me* had a dramatic conclusion: "Yes, I'll always remember. 'Till the day I die I'll hear her cry. Johnny, remember me..." This eerie hit, with its ethereal female backing voice, stayed at No. 1 for four weeks in August 1961. Leyton was a good-looking boy from Frinton-on-Sea, Essex. He wanted to be an actor, rather than a singer, but had made a big impression on record producer Joe Meek.

I had a Shadows EP (Extended Play) record for my eleventh birthday. It cost ten shillings (50p) for four tracks. My first LP (Long Player) was a Buddy Holly album that included *It doesn't matter anymore*. The second LP in this modest collection was an Everly Brothers' album including the hit *Cathy's Clown*. The third was from Eddie Cochran and included that wonderful Rock number *Somethin' Else*.

On reaching the age of 10 I became aware that kids just a few years older than me were having too much fun. I peered through the hole in our garden fence, which bordered the school playground. I could see the school hall, the venue for occasional teenage dances. There were groups playing guitars and drums. I could hear them, I could see them, but I couldn't join them. The age gap of four or five years put me firmly on the sidelines. I was too young and I lacked the confidence to go into Lee Green's record shop - which was always full of teenage girls. They were in the record booths, wearing headphones and looking cute as they moved to the music. I wondered how I could hold out until I became a teenager. Unfortunately, at least from this perspective, I was destined for Roan: a traditional, rather stern boys-only Grammar school with no room for dancing.

---ooo---

Many pop stars of the late 1950s enjoyed instant success and built a platform for successful careers that lasted decades. Others, including Buddy Holly and Eddie Cochran, tragically died young. Cliff Richard and The Shadows defied the march of time. The Shadows rode with changing musical tastes and retained a loyal following. They disbanded in 1968, re-formed in 1973, permanently disbanded in 1990 but re-formed in 2004-05 for a UK and European tour. They also re-formed again in 2008-10, to tour with Cliff Richard.

Hank Marvin had a Fender *Stratocaster*. Jet Harris had a Fender *Precision Bass*. Fame handled Harris roughly. His marriage was troubled and he suffered from depression and a drink problem. Yet he enjoyed chart success during his partnership with Tony Meehan in 1963. Hits included the outstanding *Diamonds*, with Jet Harris playing his bass as the lead instrument. The result was extremely powerful. Unfortunately, the Harris/Meehan team didn't last. By the late 1960s Jet Harris had tried a succession of jobs, from bricklayer and hospital porter to bus conductor. He was declared bankrupt in 1988. Yet he still played occasionally and started recording again in the late 1980s.

Jet Harris received the *Fender Lifetime Achievement Award* in 1998, recognising his seminal role in introducing the bass to Britain. He received another Fender award in 2010, marking the 50 years since he launched the Fender bass in the UK. Harris' own 50th anniversary in the music business was celebrated in 2007, with a tour finishing at the London Palladium. He was joined by Hank Marvin, Bruce Welch and Brian Bennett. Sadly, Harris died from cancer on 18 March, 2011. He was pre-deceased by another founder member, North Londoner Tony Meehan, who had started to play the drums at the tender age of 10. He had played alongside Jet Harris and Wally Whyton in The Vipers, before joining The Drifters in early 1959 (shortly before they became The Shadows).

Meehan became convinced that The Shadows' golden run would end quickly. In late 1961 he accepted a job as a trainee producer with Decca Records. He was present when The Beatles auditioned at Decca on 1 January, 1962. They were turned down in favour of The Tremeloes! Following his hit-making partnership with Jet Harris, Meehan returned to Decca and spent years working with bands such as The Who. He left the music industry in the 1990s to follow his lifelong interest in psychology. He became a psychologist and lecturer. Meehan died on 28 November, 2005, from head injuries suffered in a fall at home. He was just 62.

Del Shannon also died young, committing suicide on 8 February, 1990, at the age of 55. After his main chart successes he carried on singing and recording. He then became involved in production, but his life was blighted by alcoholism and depression. He shot himself with a .22 rifle at his Californian home. John Leyton's life followed a more settled pattern after his early success. His singing, acting and business talents served him well. Leyton participated in the popular *Solid Gold Rock 'n' Roll* shows, in the company of Joe Brown, Marty Wilde, Freddy Cannon and Craig Douglas.

---ooo---

I married young and my first wife's father, Dick Denney, brought the world the Vox amplifier (and much more besides). I had no idea that this incredibly inventive man, who worked with Tom Jennings of Dartford-based Jennings Musical Industries, was so close to pop megastars such as The Shadows, The Beatles and The Rolling Stones. Had I been more aware, I might have had an opportunity to meet some heroes (although Dick Denney always avoided mixing business with his private life). I was sad to learn of his death in 2001. I have fond memories of this tall, kindly man, with an evening cigar and glass of brandy and port in his hand. He called everyone, including me, "Cuz".

As a 1960s art student, I missed out on "free love", flower power and other such delights. There wasn't much of that sort of thing at Ravensbourne College of Art and Design (Vocational Annex), Wharton Road, Bromley. On the music front, we had only one interest: who was the greatest guitarist? Peter Green or Eric Clapton? This was a time when people scrawled a message on walls: "EC is God". Clapton is a wonderful musician but, clearly, this claim went too far. Both Green and Clapton played with John Mayall's Bluebreakers, a powerhouse of electric blues.

I found most music of the 1970s dull, but this changed with the Punk explosion during the second half of that decade. I saw no glamour in jumping up and down and vomiting over people, but Punk music was certainly different. It seemed to echo the energy and explosive novelty of the early Rock and Roll era. This feeling was reinforced when the Sex Pistols covered the old Eddie Cochran number, *Somethin' Else*. That really was "Somethin' else". Today, however, my tastes have changed. I listen to classical music and, in particular, "Early Music" in all its many forms. It seems that my tastes have a common thread: the music must always be different from the mainstream!

---ooo---

- 10 -

"Hello Children, Everywhere!"

Children and their parents were mesmerised by the new "goggle box". Yet the television service of the mid-1950s was limited and there were just two channels. Background noise in the home, for most of the day, was still provided by the wireless. BBC wireless services had been reorganised after the war. The Light Programme, providing popular entertainment, succeeded the General Forces Programme in July 1945. In the following year the Home Service was joined by the Third Programme, offering classical music, talks and other "serious" output.

These programmes held little interest for a 1950s 10-year-old. The teenagers in waiting tuned in to Radio Luxembourg (208m Medium Wave). Reception was far from perfect but the station's pop music programmes were hosted by the likes of Jimmy Young, Pete Murray, Simon Dee, Dave Cash and Alan Freeman – major radio and TV stars in later years.

I tuned in to 208m, "The Station of the Stars". I had to put up with religious broadcasts and commercials from programme sponsors such as the exotic Horace Batchelor, who claimed to be able to help listeners "win the Pools". The station often faded, overwhelmed by a strange, eight-note repetitive signal with a distinctly "Iron Curtain" feel. I assumed this was a Communist plot to stop us enjoying Buddy Holly, Elvis and the Everly Brothers.

---ooo---

Our 12 inch television arrived in 1956. Until then, the wireless reigned supreme. We had two radios at 48 Hedgley Street. The one in the back living room had a brown wooden cabinet and bakelite dials. It was tuned permanently to the Light Programme. Upstairs, sitting on a sideboard on the landing (I don't know why), was a larger, more ancient set. I loved to switch it on and study its wonderful illuminated dial, marked out with stations across Europe. It would hum contentedly and I liked the smell of the valves warming up.

My earliest introduction to the wireless was *Listen with Mother* (later, of course, *Watch with Mother)*. It had a 15-minute slot at 1.45 pm. The programme ran from 1952 to 1982 – at which point even the BBC had to acknowledge the commercialised destruction of childhood. Its enchanting theme (*Berceuse*, from Gabriel Fauré's *Dolly Suite*) is a time travel portal. Just a few bars are enough to return me to the past: "Are you sitting comfortably? Then I'll begin". The stories, nursery rhymes and songs were designed for under-fives and mothers. It was a great success; *Listen with Mother* had an audience exceeding one million.

My favourite programme, *Children's Favourites*, went out on Saturday morning at 9am. "Uncle Mac" (Derek McCulloch) opened with that reassuring phrase: "Hello children, everywhere!" Mum had already left for work at Oxenburghs, in Lewisham. I sneaked into the double bed, where Dad was sleeping in after his Friday night shift on the railway track. When *Children's Favourites* finished, he went into the scullery to cook bacon and tomatoes. He enjoyed this breakfast every morning, without fail, having picked up the habit in India. After returning with other starved Chindits from the Burmese jungle, he spent the next six months helping to cook breakfast for a Battalion. This was an opportunity to regain the three stone he lost during five months of fighting behind Japanese lines.

Snug under the bedclothes, we listened as Uncle Mac introduced the requests. Dad and I had two clear favourites. We sang together *The Runaway Train* and *The Big Rock Candy Mountain*. The latter was by Burl Ives and I loved one particular line: "...the bulldogs all have rubber teeth and the hens lay soft-boiled eggs..." I could also sing Burl Ives' *I know an old lady who swallowed a fly*, with its memorable chorus. *The Laughing Policeman* was played almost every week, as was *Nellie the Elephant*, *The three billy goats gruff*, *The ugly duckling*, *Old MacDonald had a farm* and *They're changing guard at Buckingham Palace*. My favourites included Mel Blanc's *I tawt I taw a puddy tat*, Doris Day's *Black Hills of Dakota*, Elton Hayes' *The Owl and the Pussycat*, Shirley Abicair's *Little boy fishing* and The Southlanders' *I am a mole and I live in a hole*.

It was impossible to escape the Max Bygraves' numbers, including *I'm a pink toothbrush, you're a blue toothbrush* and the rather strange *Gilly, Gilly Ossenfeffer, katzenellen Bogen by the sea*. I hated some frequent requests, including Rosemary Clooney's *Little Red Monkey*, Harry Belafonte's *There's a hole in my bucket, dear Liza*, Danny Kaye's *Thumbelina* and The Chipmunks' *Ragtime Cowboy Joe*. My pet hate was Charlie Drake's *My boomerang won't come back* – an emotion probably fuelled by my brother's enthusiasm for this diminutive comedian.

---ooo---

The adults also had their music programmes, including *Housewives Choice,* which was broadcast for 21 years. I was happy to go to school and miss Nat King Cole's *Mona Lisa,* Perry Como's *Catch a Falling Star,* Vic Damone's *On the street where you live* and Johnny Mathis' *Misty.* I liked Doris Day's *Que Sera, Sera, whatever will be, will be,* as Mum used to sing it to me.

Music While You Work, another long-lived programme, was launched in June 1940 to encourage millions of women on war work in the factories. It went out twice daily and continued until the Light Programme became Radio Two in 1967. The idea was to boost production by broadcasting fast-paced light music. The programme planners banned slow tunes, in case they sent people to sleep. Tunes inviting audience participation were also avoided. One casualty here was *Deep in the heart of Texas,* with its "clapping" interludes. It was thought that workers would be unable to resist the urge to bang their tools on the machines, with potentially unfortunate consequences. The programme's theme, the march *Calling All Workers,* was composed by Eric Coates. *Music While You Work* was a great success; one survey recorded a 13 per cent rise in output. The final *Music While You Work* went out on 29 September, 1967 – on the Light Programme's last day. It was revived for a week in October 1982, during the BBC's Diamond Jubilee celebrations, and was so successful that it returned to the schedules and ran daily for a year. There were also brief revivals in the early 1990s.

---oOo---

Much has been written about the boredom of Sundays in the 1950s. Much of it is true. Things were so predictable. Sunday generated a sinking feeling in the stomach and an awareness that it was school the next morning. The mood was fixed by *Two-Way Family Favourites,* the Sunday wireless programme hosted by Cliff Michelmore and Jean Metcalfe. Its signature tune – *With a Song in my Heart* – immediately conjures up the smell of boiled greens and a modest joint roasting in the oven. I had no idea what "BFPO" meant, but it was mentioned repeatedly during the programme. The content, to my young ears, was identical from one week to the next. There were occasional public service interludes, urging families with relatives who were "dangerously ill" to get in touch. It was all very depressing.

I cringed when Billy Cotton opened his Sunday show with the cry "Wakey, wakey!" Despite the band-leader's best efforts and a riotous signature tune (*Somebody Stole My Gal*), the *Billy Cotton Band Show* sent me to sleep. When the weather was bad, ruling out a visit to the park, there was always the Sunday afternoon film on TV. Otherwise, *Sing Something Simple* loomed as teatime approached and the wireless was switched on again. Our family's economic progress was charted by small changes to Sunday tea. We began with sandwiches of an up-market salmon paste, progressed to "pink salmon" and then to the real thing, "red salmon". The salmon was always spread thinly. Even today, I feel a twinge of guilt when opening a tin and eating the lot myself.

Many 1950s wireless programmes left me cold, but I took to Yorkshireman Wilfred Pickles' unmistakable voice. He started as a regional announcer, but occasionally read the Home Service news during the war. The first newsreader with a strong regional accent, he was a long way from "Received Pronunciation". Apparently, the BBC wise heads thought the Nazis would find it impossible to impersonate him. Wilfred Pickles prospered as an actor and radio personality. I remember his occasional TV appearances, but have more vivid recollections of his wireless programme *Have a Go*, which ran from 1946 to 1967. His wife, Mabel, took an active part in the shows, which were broadcast from church halls across the country. Participants shared stories with listeners and had a chance to win cash during a quiz. Pickles' famous phrases included: "How do, how are yer?" "Are yer courting?" "Give him the money, Mabel!" He had a huge audience.

There was also *Life with the Lyons*. It featured a real American family living in London. Ben Lyon, his wife, Bebe Daniels, and their two children had moved to London during the war. The couple contributed to comedian Vic Oliver's radio show *Hi, Gang!*, which ran from 1940 to 1949. Subsequently, *Life with the Lyons* was broadcast, with scripts loosely based on real events within the family.

Background noise in our home was also provided by *Beyond our Ken*, with Kenneth Horne, Kenneth Williams and Bill Pertwee, amongst others. The title played on Horne's name and the Scottish word "ken" ("understanding"). This programme ran from 1958 to 1964 and may have been very funny, although the humour sailed over my young head. My only recollection is of a Kenneth Williams' character, the gardener "Arthur Fallowfield". He deflected all questions with the comment: "The answer lies in the soil", a phrase that penetrated the national consciousness.

---ooo---

The 1960s radio revolution dawned with the offshore pirate stations and non-stop pop music from Radio Caroline and Radio London. The new DJs, including Kenny Everett, took the public by storm. When the Government closed down the pirates in the late 1960s, British broadcasting could not keep to its old ways. Programming was re-organised. Radio One was meant to fill the void left by the demise of the pirates. The Light Programme became Radio Two and the Third Programme emerged as Radio Three (a bastion of civilisation to this day). The Home Service became Radio Four, its programme content and quality stoutly defended by listeners who are inherently resistant to change. God bless them!

In 1960, however, this revolution was still some years away. The Light Programme's content had changed little since the early 1950s. It offered a proven mix of light music, comedy and drama. The Light Programme opened at 6.34am with *Morning Music*, followed by *The Band Plays On* and *Housewives' Choice*. Programmes during the day included *Music While You Work*, *Mrs Dale's Diary*, *The Ted Heath Show*, *Woman's Hour*, *The Archers* and *Educating Archie*. Broadcasting ended at midnight. Two of these programmes, *The Archers* and *Woman's Hour*, are likely to outlive most of us.

Uncle Mac hosted his last *Children's Favourites* in 1965. Following the 1967 reorganisation *Children's Favourites* became *Junior Choice*, hosted by Ed "Stewpot" Stewart for 11 years. Surprisingly, many "Uncle Mac" favourites continued to be requested - almost certainly by nostalgic parents, rather than their children.

I have a friend who has a CD of Uncle Mac's *Children's Favourites*. The power of the old songs is quite remarkable. Somehow they seem to speak of the profound changes of the past 50 years. As for adult programming, *Family Favourites* soldiered on in its Radio Two slot until 1980. Cliff Michelmore and Jean Metcalfe were succeeded by Michael Aspel and Sarah Kennedy.

Uncle Mac died in 1967. Wilfred Pickles died in 1978. *Beyond our Ken* was succeeded in 1965 by *Round the Horne*, another play on the programme anchor's name. The skill of writers Barry Took and Marty Feldman, together with most of the *Beyond our Ken* ensemble, filled the new show with sexual innuendo and *double entendres*. It passed over my head at the time. I suppose I would find it extremely funny now. The galaxy of characters included Kenneth Williams' "J. Peasemold Gruntfuttock" (the "world's dirtiest old man") and "Julian" and "Sandy" – Hugh Paddick and Kenneth Williams playing two gay out-of-work actors using *Polari* slang. Homosexual behaviour was still a criminal offence at the time. They got away with it because only a very few understood what Williams *et al* were actually talking about. The vast majority of listeners, including, presumably, the BBC Governors, were probably content as it sounded funny, anyway!

Many radio comedy shows had long lives. *The Navy Lark*, concerning the frigate HMS Troutbridge and all who sailed in her, ran from 1959 to 1977. The cast included Leslie Phillips, Jon Pertwee, Ronnie Barker and Dennis Price. The theme was the hornpipe *St Ninian's Isle*. This show gave the nation several catchphrases, including "Left hand down a bit" and "You're rotten, you are!"

---ooo---

I came along just too late to enjoy the golden age of wireless. Yet I have strong memories of *Journey into Space*, broadcast from 1953 to 1958. I was not alone in my fascination with Jet Morgan, Lemmy (the spaceship's radio operator) and the dramatic noise of the rocket launch that opened each episode. Apparently, Stephen Hawking was a fan.

Meanwhile, real scientific advances began to intrude into our lives. The first transistor was developed by Bell Laboratories in 1947. A prototype transistor radio was demonstrated in June 1948; millions were manufactured. The first commercial transistor radio was the Regency TR-1, from American producers Texas Instruments and Industrial Development Engineering Association. The first British transistor radio was launched by Pye in 1956. For the first time, the public had "music on the move".

---ooo---

– II –

"Are You Sitting Comfortably?"

BBC Television began in the 1930s but closed for the duration of the war. Broadcasting resumed in June 1946. With the passage of the years, it is difficult to explain just how enthusiastic people were towards television when it first became affordable. The 1950s television set was a status symbol. Proud owners soon discovered they had a larger than expected circle of friends. Visitors arrived clutching the thinnest of excuses, in the hope that the set would be turned on. The kids next door dropped in to watch children's programmes.

Our first set was housed in a tall wooden cabinet. It gave a faint hum of satisfaction when turned on. This was followed by the glow, visible through the slots in the back, and the smell of warming valves. A bright dot appeared in the centre of the 12 inch screen and slowly expanded. Everyone was overwhelmed by this amazing device and the Coronation, in June 1953, gave television a major boost. Our roofs soon sprouted a rash of TV aerials (all H-shaped).

Television within reach: a 17 inch model offered for rental by DER. The Redding family's first television was earlier and had a 12 inch screen.

The Television Bill 1954 created the Independent Television Authority and ITV's first programmes were broadcast in September 1955. BBC TV programmes, meanwhile, changed little during the 1950s. In 1960 the typical Wednesday fare included the *Flowerpot Men*, *Prudence Kitten*, *Tonight* (with Cliff Michelmore, Derek Hart, Alan Whicker and Fyfe Robertson – famed for his Deerstalker hat), *Wells Fargo* (starring Dale Robertson) and a young Patrick Moore with the indestructible *The sky at Night*. The news and weather, at 10.45 pm, was followed by *Evening Prayers* and closedown. The picture shrank to a bright shrinking dot when the TV set was turned off.

I found it difficult to wait for programmes to start. The "Test Card" appeared a few minutes before the programmes began. The TV Newsreel's introduction was exciting, with Alexandra Palace's mast emitting "TV waves" to a brisk musical theme. It was pure magic! Things often went wrong: most programmes were live and technical problems were commonplace. Breakdowns were acknowledged by a "Technical Fault" apology card and one of the BBC's large stock of interlude shorts (the *Potter's Wheel* was the most memorable). I came to trust that famous BBC promise: "Normal service will be resumed as soon as possible". I always felt they were doing their best.

Television broadcasting at that time had a gentlemanly feel. The same could be said of early TV commercials. A small, bakelite-cased device allowed us to receive ITV. The station's most popular programmes included *Emergency Ward 10*, *The Army Game* and *Criss Cross Quiz*. There was also *Junior Criss Cross Quiz*.

Camera 2: the author's late father-in-law, Stan Boylett, worked for the BBC for many years and was involved in many famous programmes, from Tonight to Dad's Army.

Mum had the bright idea of entering me as a contestant. She felt this would be a good dry run for my 11-Plus exam. We travelled to London and I took a seat in a small room crowded with other hopefuls (probably also dragged there by their parents). When it was my turn for assessment I was unlucky with the questions. Mum received a polite letter announcing my rejection. This was probably all to the good. Fifty years later, I occasionally appear on television. Several people have commented that the camera does not flatter me – I have a "radio face" and, sadly, lack a "radio voice".

---ooo---

Adventure series, especially westerns, dominated 1950s' children's television. Popular series included *The Lone Ranger* (with Tonto), *The Cisco Kid* (with Pancho), *Range Rider* and the definitive US Cavalry programme, *Boots and Saddles*. Westerns aimed at an adult audience, such as *Wagon Train* and *Rawhide*, were also loved by kids.

British adventure series focused on "historical figures" such as Robin Hood, Sir Lancelot, Ivanhoe and William Tell. Richard Greene's 1950s *Robin Hood* enthralled kids and, no doubt, accidents involving toy bows and arrows increased as a result. I really liked *Sir Lancelot* (all that shiny tin armour). Dad loved Gessler, William Tell's arch enemy.

I hated popular quiz programmes such as *Take Your Pick* and *Double Your Money* (hosted by Michael Miles and Hughie Green, respectively). I preferred that old-fashioned policeman George Dixon (*Dixon of Dock Green*) and *The Army Game* was hilarious. My favourite character was William Hartnell, who played "Sergeant-Major Bullimore". I detested *The Black and White Minstrel Show*, but loved Professor Jimmy Edwards in *Whack-O!* It was good to watch boys being beaten so ruthlessly. Equally, I found the kids' programmes *Blue Peter* and *Crackerjack* patronising and dull.

---ooo---

"It's tingling fresh. It's fresh as ice. It's Gibbs SR toothpaste". At 8.12 pm on 22 September, 1955, this toothpaste commercial was the first to be broadcast. The honour came as a matter of random chance: *Gibbs SR* was drawn from 23 other commercials, including *Surf* soap powder, *Guinness* and *Summer County* margarine. *Summer County* had a taste nothing like butter yet was quite palatable.

I don't remember the *Gibbs SR* commercial, but vividly recall another: "You'll wonder where the yellow went, when you brush your teeth with Pepsodent."

The extraordinary power of television commercials soon became apparent. Some early "jingles" are still firmly embedded in my mind, even to this day. There was that atmospheric music for a cigarette commercial – "You're never alone with a Strand" (1959). The solitary, trench-coated man stood on a dark street and lit up. The public lit up in sympathy. *The lonely man* theme was recorded by Cliff Adams.

Sweets and drinks were well represented: "Murray Mints, Murray Mints... too good to hurry mints" and "Coates comes up from Somerset, where the cider apples grow". Some popular themes, such as the *Brooke Bond PG Tips* chimps, came to be regarded as politically incorrect in later years.

Many commercials got under the skin. They included the "Go to work on an egg" campaign, with Tony Hancock. There was Joe, the cartoon *Esso Blue* paraffin salesman with a speech impediment (he was the "Esso Blee Dooler"). *Esso* also produced a TV jingle that was almost impossible to drive from the mind: "Oh, the Esso sign means happy motoring. The Esso sign means happy motoring. The Esso sign means happy motoring. Call at the Esso sign!" I quite liked a light bulb commercial, with its characters "Flashy" and "Dim".

Housewives who wished to stay married studied Katie, the *OXO* lady who satisfied her husband by producing gallons of dark brown gravy. If only things were that simple! Many later campaigns were to exploit family relationships and the ability of some products to assist in the blossoming and maintenance of love.

Ribena had a commercial which, to the modern mind, plays on the wrong part of the word blackcurrant. Many slogans entered the public mind, such as "Don't just say brown, say Hovis". Bernard Miles, in his unique way, said *Mackeson* "looks good, tastes good and, by golly, it does you good". Apparently, my Nan agreed, frequently despatching me to the off-licence with half-a-crown, to fetch her next bottle of stout ("...and look sharp about it!").

Soap powder commercials were boring, featuring dummy housewives (or, perhaps, just dummies) and the inevitable "Brand X". Ludicrous challenges were made, such as "Can you tell Stork from butter?" Regardless of *Stork's* relative merits, even a silicon-based lifeform from the Tau Ceti star system could make this distinction. I preferred *Sugar Frosties* and Tony the Tiger: "They're grrrrreat". My Dad's favourite was the battery slogan "I told 'em, Oldham". For some reason he found this immensely funny. Technological progress was evident in products such as the *Little X* corselette, with its "ten tiny panels – like ten little fingers – at each side of the garment, continually massaging your stomach and ensuring that it is held in and kept flat, all at the same time". This sounds like a heavy price to pay for looking marginally slimmer.

---ooo---

"Are you sitting comfortably? Then I'll begin". Viewers received a gentle welcome to the world of *Watch with Mother*, populated by *Andy Pandy* (with rag doll Looby Loo and Teddy), *The Flowerpot Men* (with Weed) and *Rag, Tag and Bobtail* ("Hello Rag, hello Tag, hello Bobtail!"). There was *Whirligig*, with Mr Turnip, Hank the Cowboy ("Howdy folks") and bandit Mexican Pete. Hank was goofy, but not as goofy as his horse, "Old Timer". The flavour may be gauged from other characters: "Little He-He", the son of "Big Chief Laughing Gas", and "Minnie Ha-Ha". *Whirlygig* launched Rolf Harris' long television career.

That awful puppet *Muffin the Mule*, the butt of a billion pub jokes, starred in the earliest kids' programme. *For the Children* was broadcast when television resumed after the war. Children's Television took off in 1950 with *Watch with Mother* – developed by Freda Lingstrom, later Head of BBC Children's Television. Andy Pandy's first appearance was on 11 July, 1950. He lived in a picnic basket (which, it seems to me, is a fine address). Just 26 episodes were made and they were repeated endlessly throughout the 1950s.

In 1952 *The Flowerpot Men* popped up for the first time, filling *Watch with Mother's* Wednesday slot. Bill and Ben had flowerpot bodies, gardening glove hands and hobnailed boots for feet. They lived in two gigantic flowerpots and surfaced – with the assistance of string – whenever the gardener went for something to eat. Weed kept vigil as the Flowerpot Men got up to their tricks, watched by Slowcoach the tortoise. The episodes were virtually identical. When something went wrong the guilty party was sought: "Which of those two Flowerpot Men? Was it Bill or was it Ben?" With the culprit exposed, the gardener returned and the Flowerpot Men disappeared. Only Weed and the little house at the bottom of the garden had any inkling of what had gone on.

Bill and Ben communicated in *Oddle Poddle,* which consisted of "Flibadobs", "Flobadobs" and nonsensical questions. This language has interesting origins. Three Bill and Ben stories were written for the *Listen with Mother* wireless programme by Hilda Brabbon. They were based on earlier tales written for her younger brothers, William and Benjamin. Whenever the two were naughty, their mother would demand: "Was it Bill or was it Ben?" Apparently, "Flobadob" was the word the boys used when farting in the bath.

My favourite was *Rag, Tag and Bobtail*, occupying the Thursday slot and featuring a hedgehog, mouse and rabbit. *The Woodentops* came a little later, in 1955. I didn't think much of it, with the exception of Spotty Dog – much mimicked, with that peculiar, strangled bark and robotic style of walking.

---ooo---

Christmas at the studios: callers brave the "snow". Dispensing snowflakes, on the right, is "Bunny" Boylett, my wife's Uncle, who spent many years with the BBC.

Television Westerns dominated during the 1950s. Back from school, I would settle into the armchair with two crusty rolls (cheddar cheese and corned beef) to watch *The Lone Ranger*, *The Cisco Kid* or *Range Rider*. I looked forward to the evening and *Gunsmoke*, *Wagon Train* and *Rawhide*.

For reasons which now escape me, I never went to Saturday morning pictures. I missed ancient cowboy films starring Audie Murphy, Hopalong Cassidy, Tom Mix and singing cowboys Roy Rogers and Gene Autry. Television Westerns were good enough for me, including *The Lone Ranger*, with his mask, fancy outfit, companion Tonto and a wonderful horse called Silver. I tried not to miss episodes of *The Cisco Kid* and *Range Rider* ("with all-American boy Dick West!"). Their horses were fantastic, appearing to gallop at around 60 mph without a sweat. *Range Rider* was a typical 30-minute "oater". A total of 79 programmes were made during the 1951-1953 period and the series reached British audiences a few years later.

The Cisco Kid starred in a 1907 short story (*The Caballero's way*) about a ruthless killer. This bandit evolved into a hero and featured in a popular American radio series from 1947 to 1956. The signature ending, with the characters calling "Oh, Pancho!"... "Oh, Cisco!" before riding off at the gallop, laughing, continued in the TV series (1950—1956) – the first to be filmed in colour.

Champion the Wonder Horse was a magnificent animal, but I preferred *Rin Tin Tin*, the German Shepherd belonging to orphan boy Rusty, who lived on a US Cavalry post. Far superior, however, was *Boots and Saddles*, with its dramatic opening sequence and pounding theme. This was quite unlike any other TV Western. The mood was grim and the soldiers were always hot, thirsty, dusty and wide awake to the dangers of life as a frontier cavalryman. The series, filmed in Utah, portrayed the Fifth Cavalry and ran from 1957 to 1959. The 39 episodes were not enough.

I also liked *Whiplash*, a Western with a difference. Britain's Independent Television Corporation had successfully sold historical swashbucklers into America and wanted a successful Western. It was decided to set the new series in Australia. The outcome was the Australian Western *Whiplash*, based (albeit loosely) on the adventures of Cobb & Co. Stagecoach Lines – set up by Freeman Cobb in 1853. His stagecoach empire was built on the busy runs between Melbourne and the goldfields of Victoria and the Cobb network eventually spread across Eastern Australia. Some scripts were written by Gene Roddenberry, *Star Trek's* creator. Peter Graves, brother of *Gunsmoke* actor James Arness, played the lead. Graves also played Jim Phelps in *Mission Impossible*. *Whiplash*, first broadcast in September 1960, had a theme sung by Frank Ifield: "In 1851, the Great Australian Gold Rush. The only law a gun, the only shelter wild bush... Whiplash, Whiplash..." The real Cobb & Co. ran its last coach in 1924 – lasting somewhat longer than the television series.

Wagon Train and *Rawhide* were classic Westerns with memorable catchphrases: "Wagons... ho!" and "Head 'em up, move 'em out!" *Wagon Train* has its origins in the 1950 John Ford film *Wagon Master*. There was also an earlier wagon train film, *The Big Trail* (1930), which, coincidentally, gave Ward Bond his first major role.

Wagon Train ran from 1957 to 1965 and told the story of pioneers on the trail from Missouri to California. The wagon train was commanded by Major Seth Adams, played in blunt, golden-hearted style by Ward Bond. He was supported by his Scout, the young Confederate Army veteran Flint McCullough (Robert Horton). Ward Bond had a heart attack and died in late 1960, aged just 57 and only three years into the hit show's eight-year run. His death was big news and newspapers mused: who would now lead the pioneers west? The new Wagon Master was the highly experienced John McIntire, who played Christopher Hale, with Robert Fuller as Scout "Coop" (Cooper Smith). Fuller had played Jess Harper in the successful series *Laramie*.

Agents vied for a guest spot on *Wagon Train*. There were 284 episodes and the guest stars included Bette Davis, Peter Lorre, Lee Marvin, Leonard Nimoy (with "regular" ears), Mickey Rooney and Ronald Reagan (in a late acting role before commencing the political career which eventually took him to the White House).

Wagon Train was set in the years immediately after the Civil War, when the plains tribes still opposed the white tide heading west. Seth Adams and his successor drew the wagons into a defensive circle for the night. The wagons used in the series were short versions of the Conestoga *Prairie Schooner*, which was usually drawn by oxen rather than horses. The programme held its audience by exploiting the unknown. What was behind the next pass or the next river crossing? Some programmes vividly portrayed the hardships of trail life. One harrowing episode featured the sole survivor of a doomed wagon train, trapped in a snow-blocked mountain pass. It was implied that he had survived by eating his dead companions. In fact, there are well-documented cases of a handful of emaciated survivors rescued in the Spring thaw, their shelters filled with grisly remains.

Rawhide also had a long run, from 1959 to 1966. It was the fifth longest running American Western series (*Wagon Train*, eight years; *The Virginian*, nine years; *Bonanza*, 14 years; and *Gunsmoke*, the champion at 20 years). *Rawhide* starred the young Clint Eastwood as "Ramrod" Rowdy Yates, with Trail Boss Gil Favor played to perfection by Eric Fleming. There was also Sheb Wooley as Favor's original Scout, Pete Nolan, and Paul Brinegar as that unforgettable cook Wishbone.

Rawhide had every ingredient necessary for a successful Western. The drovers took 3,000 head of cattle from San Antonio, Texas, along the trail to Sedalia, Missouri. Later, Favor took his herds on the Chisum Trail. He was responsible for a fortune, with the beef valued at well over one million dollars in today's terms. The cattle were drawn from the stock of around 200 owners and his drovers received one dollar a day, plus vittels. They took turns "riding drag" – bringing up the rear, in the herd's thick dust cloud.

Filmed in black and white, *Rawhide* had a bleak, austere feel. Gil Favor was a natural leader and it was obvious that Eric Fleming loved the role. The series' authenticity is due in part to Producer Charles Warren's use of an 1866 diary written by Trail Boss George C. Duffield, who drove a herd from San Antonio to Sedalia and provided the model for Gil Favor. His TV reincarnation had plenty to contend with, from wolves and murderers to smallpox and "ghost-riders". Every move Favor made was dominated by his constant need to stay within reach of sufficient water. I remember one especially eerie episode, when the herd's horns were lit by St Elmo's Fire.

The list of guest stars in this series makes remarkable reading: Mary Astor, Charles Bronson, Broderick Crawford, Robert Culp, Buddy Ebsen, Frankie Laine, Peter Lorre, Burgess Meredith and Barbara Stanwyck, to name just a few. Frankie Laine had a hit with the *Rawhide* theme. *Rawhide's* great star met a sad end, just after the series finished. Eric Fleming drowned in 1966, when his canoe rolled over during filming. He was only 41.

---ooo---

How did Robert Newton manage to create such a marvellous *Long John Silver*, with those rolling eyes and salty exclamations ("A...haar, there!")? With "Young Jim", "Patch" and "Purrrity" (Long John's buxom love interest), the pirate supremo sailed through his amazing adventures without a scratch (although, of course, minus a limb). His crutch, a versatile weapon, often crashed down on the heads of those being awkward.

I loved the *Long John Silver* theme song: "Sixteen men on a dead man's chest, yo, ho, ho and a bottle of rum! Drink and the Devil have done with the rest. Yo, ho, ho and a bottle of rum!" I could imitate Long John's sayings, including "Avast, there!" and "Belay that!" Grown-ups must have found it odd that a seven-year-old boy should suddenly demand: "Purrrity...hand me my grog!" when asking for the custard jug. Sadly, I lacked a parrot. If I had a parrot it would have been called Captain Flint. I would have trained it to screech "Pieces of Eight!"

Long John Silver, of course, is the central character in Robert Louis Stevenson's *Treasure Island*. Silver had been Captain Flint's Quartermaster and claimed to have lost a leg in action with the Royal Navy. By nature, Long John is a blackguard (to slip into appropriate language). He always looked for the advantage, especially when treasure was involved.

Robert Newton made two *Long John Silver* films and 26 episodes of the immortal TV series. It was made in Australia, for broadcast in the USA and UK. Connie Gilchrist played Purity Pinker and Kit Taylor was young Jim Hawkins, brave yet bedazzled by Long John and the romance of the pirate lifestyle. The pirates included Grant Taylor as Patch and Billy Kay as Ironhand.

During my life I have had occasion to borrow one of Long John's favourite sayings: "Arrrr...females!" Whilst watching this series, all those years ago, I had no idea that my hero was already dead. Newton suffered a fatal heart attack before the programme was first screened in Britain.

Another favourite, on late Saturday afternoons, was *The Adventures of Sir Lancelot* (1956—1957), starring William Russell as Sir Lancelot du Lac. The plots benefited from the contributions of Oxford University academics prominent in the fields of history and literature, yet were hopelessly wrong in historical context. It focused on the 14th-century world of chivalry, rather than the Dark Age reality of Arthur (if, indeed, there was an Arthur). Such trifles were of no concern as I watched my hero save damsels in distress and fight with lance and sword. At that time, of course, I had no idea that one of the central themes of Arthurian legend is the treacherous sexual relationship between Sir Lancelot and Queen Guinevere.

Sir Lancelot was produced by Sapphire Films, the company also responsible for perhaps the greatest of the 1950s TV swashbucklers, *The Adventures of Robin Hood*. This starred Richard Greene, wearing the best tailored suit of Lincoln Green this side of Sherwood Forest. *Robin Hood*, an early ITV show, had a tremendous following. Everyone of a certain age can still sing the theme: "Robin Hood, Robin Hood, riding through the glen. Robin Hood, Robin Hood, with his band of men. Feared by the bad, loved by the good. Robin Hood, Robin Hood, Robin Hood". I adored the opening sequence. The whoosh of the arrow certainly conveyed the incredible power of the longbow (to which many a French Knight might have testified, had they survived Agincourt and Crecy).

Robin Hood was screened from 1955 to 1960, in 143 episodes. There was something essentially decent about Richard Greene's Robin Hood, perhaps coloured by the officer class of two world wars ("Thanks awfully, old chap!"). Archie Duncan was memorable as Little John – not particularly bright but certainly loyal. The real man was not short on courage. Archie Duncan was injured on set when heavy scenery began to fall on some children. He pushed them out of the way and took the blow himself. It broke his leg. Subsequently, Little John received the *Queen's Commendation for Bravery*.

Other memorable characters included Alexander Gauge as Friar Tuck, a victim of good food but handy with the Quarterstaff when called upon to fight. Paul Eddington played Will Scarlet. The first Maid Marion (Lady Marion Fitzwalter) was played by Irish actress Bernadette O'Farrell, but my memories are of her gorgeous successor, Patricia Driscoll. She may have had a less aristocratic take on the character, but was unbearably cute when peeking out from behind a tree. The series was set at a time when there was something seriously wrong with England. King Richard was absent, John was a tyrant and the Sheriff of Nottingham was John's willing accomplice. Abbots were wealthy and greedy. Peasants were oppressed and justice, of a kind, resided only in the Greenwood. Alan Wheatley was masterful as the dastardly Sheriff, although, of course, he was thwarted at every turn by the boys in green.

Clever production techniques were used. Props, from a baronial fireplace to a fallen tree, were mounted on wheels and an entire set could be changed within six minutes. This was masterminded by Artistic Director Peter Proud, who had been a wartime camouflage expert. The "chain mail" of the Sheriff's men consisted of knotted string sprayed silver. Guest stars included Thora Hird, Nicholas Parsons, Sid James, Jane Asher, Irene Handl, Wilfred Bramble, Harry H. Corbett and Bill Owen.

In sharp contrast to *Robin Hood*, people were seen to die in *William Tell*. Dad and I regarded this as the best of the swashbucklers – from David Whitfield's stirring rendition of Rossini's *William Tell Overture* to the disgusting Landburgher Gessler. He roared "Bring me Tell" whilst throwing a half-eaten chicken leg from his podgy, greasy fingers. We resented Gessler, as we rarely had chicken at our table. Conrad Phillips put on a sheepskin to play William Tell and stoutly resist the savage Austrian occupation. Willoughby Goddard made the perfect Gessler – a part played with as much gusto as Robert Newton played Long John Silver. There were 39 episodes over the 1958—59 period. The production budget did not stretch to filming in Switzerland, but North Wales was a passable substitute.

---oOo---

I loved cartoons, especially *Popeye the Sailor*. Popeye first appeared in a 1929 comic strip. He started out as a minor character but won rapid promotion, propelled by those muscular forearms, an addiction to strength-giving spinach, deep love for Olive Oyl and bitter hatred of his *bête noire*, the bearded hulk Bluto. There was also J. Wellington Wimpy, pre-occupied with eating hamburgers. Sweetpea, a foundling baby who arrived by post in 1933, completed the characters.

These cartoons were made from the early 1930s and continued in production until 1957. Popeye became Hollywood's most popular cartoon character. There were only a few plot lines – everything was predictable and immensely enjoyable. Bluto would bid for Olive's hand and Popeye would struggle to see him off. Olive revelled in the attentions of both. She became starry-eyed whenever expensive gifts were proffered (especially jewellery), yet her true allegiance was suggested by her crooning song: "I want a clean-shaven man". My favourite moment came when Popeye, his back to the wall, consumed a can of spinach (sometimes sucking it in through his pipe) and obtained instant results. He tensed his biceps and exploding atomic bombs appeared. There was no doubt about the efficacy of spinach!

Popeye cartoons opened with *The Sailor's Hornpipe*, followed by the theme song "I'm Popeye the sailor man". His catchphrase was: "I yam what I yam and that's all what I yam". When Popeye blew a fuse (in a situation usually requiring a spinach fix), he would declare: "That's all I can stands. I can't stands no more!" God help Bluto or other opponents, such as the "Goons" of Goon Island, an unpleasant race of robotic humanoids. In his early days Popeye increased US spinach consumption by one third, prompting the spinach-growers of Crystal City, Texas, to erect a statue in his honour.

As the late 1950s became the early 1960s, I enjoyed *Boss Cat* – known to most kids by the original title *Top Cat*. The cartoons featured the alley cats led by "TC". Always looking for a free ride, they were often frustrated by killjoy police officer Charlie Dibble. The characters were well drawn and amusing: "Brains, Benny, Choo-Choo". The cats came to realise that Officer Dibble wasn't such a bad guy after all.

---oOo---

I was taken to the Doctors at the age of five. Mum was concerned about my frequent vivid nightmares. I had frightening dreams about lions and tigers. Dr

Tangney listened sympathetically and suggested that no picturebooks should be looked at after 5 pm. A couple of years later, however, TV gave me something else to have nightmares about: *The Trollenberg Terror*. This six-part ITV serial was shown on Saturdays during 1956. It scared the living daylights out of me! The plot was simplicity itself: a succession of unexplained, horrific deaths had occurred in the Austrian Alps. The culprits were hostile aliens, hiding in the cloud-covered upper slopes of the Trollenberg peak. I couldn't stop watching it, but found it hard to sleep afterwards.

Equally scary was *The Voodoo Factor*, another Saturday serial. Its six episodes were broadcast from 12 December, 1959, to 16 January, 1960. Maurice Kaufman starred as Dr David Whittaker, a tropical disease specialist. He confronts a Polynesian spider goddess cult with plans to spread a deadly virus across the world. *The Voodoo Factor* had an especially effective opening sequence.

Perhaps my parents allowed me to watch *The Trollenberg Terror, The Voodoo Factor* and similar fare to toughen me up and prevent regression into nightmares about lions and tigers. If so, I have them to thank for a lifelong interest in science fiction of a certain type (what I would describe as the quality end of the market – Clifford Simak, Eric Frank Russell, Ray Bradbury, et al). This was the age of Cold War paranoia and science fiction enjoyed a boom. Notable television science fiction during the 1950s included Professor Bernard Quatermass and his various adventures. *The Quatermass Experiment* (1953), *Quatermass II* (1955) and *Quatermass and the pit* (1958-59) scared the wits out of a lot of adults, let alone the kids. These programmes passed me by. We had no television in 1953 and the later serials were deemed "unsuitable". I can't say I'm sorry, given my over-active imagination!

Reginald Tate played rocket scientist Professor Quatermass as a peculiarly British hero, squaring up to a deadly threat to humanity from hostile aliens. The character's first name was a tribute to British astronomer Bernard Lovell. The first series concerned a manned rocket that crash-landed in London, with an alien presence on board. It became a Saturday night hit of huge proportions, even emptying pubs! According to the British Film Institute, *The Quatermass Experiment* was one of the most influential television series of the 1950s. In *Quatermass II* the Professor presses on regardless, planning bases on the Moon. In *Quatermass and the pit* the Professor, once again, saves the world from aliens.

If *Quatermass* was *verboten*, watching *Space Patrol* was a self-inflicted wound. God knows what I was doing watching this puppet series at the age of 14. *Space Patrol* was an oddball when first broadcast in 1963. I should have been more interested in The Beatles and Rolling Stones! *Space Patrol* was created by Roberta Leigh and Arthur Provis, who had worked with Gerry and Sylvia Anderson – the makers of several very successful puppet series. *Space Patrol* featured voice-synchronised marionettes with a way of moving that can only be described as awkward. Captain Larry Dart and his crew, a Venusian and a Martian, seemed to have broken their hips. Yet, there was something about this show and its "spinning top" ship, Galasphere 347. Anything with a top speed of one million miles an hour has to be good! The programme made atmospheric use of strange electronic music. The opening theme was memorable, as was the closing sequence, with its futuristic cityscape. Best of all, however, was the stilted dialogue: "All in order, Captain!" "Meson Power on!" All my life, I have longed for access to Meson Power. Mesons do exist but, sadly, no-one has yet found a way to harness them for interstellar travel.

My fascination with "social" science fiction grew by watching an outstanding American series, *The Twilight Zone*. The original series ran from 1959 to 1964 (156 episodes). There were two revivals (1985-89 and 2002-03). *The Twilight Zone* was created by Rod Serling, who was passionate about the big issues, from war and racism to abuse of power and the foibles of human nature. *The Twilight Zone* gave him a platform to air these issues at a time when social commentary was regarded as far too contentious for mainstream TV.

The Twilight Zone had a highly successful formula: a science fiction or fantasy story delivered with an opening narration by Serling and ending with a twist and a closing narration. A number of leading science fiction writers contributed, including Ray Bradbury and Richard Matheson, but many episodes came from Serling's own hand. He was that rare man, who knew exactly what he wanted to say and how best to say it. Sharp social comment was folded into a drama, to evade censorship by sponsors and networks. Programme themes were often allegorical, exploring nuclear war, the power of mass hysteria and the paranoia of the McCarthy period. Serling even took to popping up in the middle of episodes to make his point (the characters apparently unaware of his presence).

Serling's main message was that the guilty must pay. Typically, the stories followed people leading ordinary lives who suddenly find themselves propelled into extraordinary situations: "You are about to enter another dimension. A dimension not only of sight and sound, but of mind. A journey into a wondrous land of imagination. Next stop, the Twilight Zone!" That journey took viewers into a world rich in fear, comedy, pathos, prejudice and surprise. Actors making the journey included Burt Reynolds, Dennis Hopper, Robert Redford, Charles Bronson, James Coburn, Mickey Rooney and even Buster Keaton.

The Twilight Zone was followed by *The Outer Limits* (1963—65), a science fiction series of 49 episodes. Vic Perrin's *Control Voice* introduced and concluded each episode, often hammering home a philosophical point or two. The introduction was masterful: "There is nothing wrong with your television set. Do not attempt to adjust the picture. We are controlling the transmission. We will control the horizontal. We will control the vertical. You are about to participate in a great adventure. You are about to experience the awe and mystery which reaches from the inner mind to The Outer Limits." Early episodes featured the "monster of the week". Later episodes took a more mature approach. Nevertheless, creatures continued to make guest appearances. Some were so scary that a few American TV stations blacked out the monster sequences, to avoid giving their viewers seizures.

The Twilight Zone told its story in the form of a parable. *The Outer Limits* was more straightforward. It had an atmospheric, brooding quality, with episodes dealing with themes such as alien takeover and abduction. Its eerie atmosphere had a sense of *film noir*. This series fared less well than *The Twilight Zone*, perhaps due to its more radical format. I loved both and watched as many episodes as possible.

Later, the BBC screened *Out of the Unknown*, broadcast over the 1965-1971 period. The 49 episodes dramatised science fiction short stories. By this time I had read all the science fiction I could lay my hands on. I was familiar with most storylines from contributing authors to an earlier series, *Out of this world* (1962). They included some big names, such as Isaac Asimov, Philip K. Dick and John Wyndham. The first episode of *Out of the unknown*, broadcast in October 1965, was an adaptation of John Wyndham's "No place like Earth". The first series became the most popular BBC2 drama after *The Virginian*. Successive series continued to broadcast high quality work from authors such as Robert Sheckley, John Brunner and Clifford D. Simak.

Of all the early televised science fiction, I have fondest memories of Fred Hoyle and John Elliot's *A for Andromeda* (1961), with the beautiful Julie Christie – then a drama student – taking the main role. The storyline was mind-boggling (at least to this 12-year-old). A scientific establishment receives digital signals from space which provide a blueprint for the construction of a super-computer. Instructions are then given for the creation of "Andromeda" (a fetching clone of Julie Christie, a member of the scientific team until killed off in the main computer room). Andromeda is a tool for an alien takeover. Each episode opened with a clever device: a "television interview" with Professor Ernst Reinhart (played by Esmond Knight), who reviewed developments so far. The messages were received by a new British radio telescope under Reinhart's control. Government and military attempts to harness Andromeda for defence and industrial purposes came to nothing. In short, the computer is destroyed and Andromeda dies.

Hoyle's inspiration for *A for Andromeda* was astronomer Frank Drake (who wrote the famous "ET equation" – a formula for estimating how many civilisations might exist in the universe). At that time Drake was involved in "SETI" (the Search for Extra-Terrestrial Intelligence). The TV series was an outstanding success, attracting an audience peaking at nearly 13 million. Newspapers of the time felt obliged to remind viewers that DNA – a relatively recent discovery – was real! A sequel, *The Andromeda breakthrough*, was made in 1962. Apparently, the BBC had refused to pay £300 to retain Julie Christie and Susan Hampshire took her part. Amusingly, the Swiss scientific group featured in both series was known as "Intel".

---oOo---

Crime drama became increasingly popular in the early 1950s. A quintessentially British programme was *Fabian of the Yard*, based on the real experiences of Robert Fabian, a Scotland Yard detective. This BBC series of 36 episodes was broadcast between late 1954 and early 1956. I can still picture the distinctive face of Bruce Seton, who played the intrepid Fabian. His cases made good drama; each episode was based on a real crime and Seton provided the voiceover narration. At the close, the image of Seton at his desk faded into the real Fabian, sitting at the very same desk, who then related what had happened to the criminal or criminals. It was satisfying to hear that they had got their just desserts.

My favourite British crime series starred Raymond Francis, who played Detective Superintendent Tom Lockhart in *Murder Bag* (1957—59). It was clear that the game was up when Lockhart knocked on your door. The Murder Bag was the forensic kit first developed for use at crime scenes by forensic pathologist Sir Bernard Spilsbury. Lockhart's taciturn manner lent realism to the 55 episodes. I loved those black *Wolseley* police cars, fitted with bells rather than sirens. Bells, somehow, are more British.

Raymond Francis was promoted after *Murder Bag*. He became Detective Chief Superintendent Lockhart for the later *Crime Sheet* series of 17 programmes (of which, sadly, I remember nothing). Fortunately, I do have clear memories of the subsequent series, *No Hiding Place* (1959—67). Lockhart received no more promotion – any rank above Chief Superintendent would mean that he would no longer personally attend crime scenes. Lockhart was assisted by Eric Lander as

Detective Inspector Harry Baxter and a pre-*Coronation Street* Johnny Briggs as Detective Sergeant Russell.

No hiding place was a triumph of realism through attention to detail. Glyn Davies, a former Scotland Yard detective, served as series consultant. A total of 236 episodes were made. An attempt to scrap the series in 1965 met with fierce public and police protests; it was extended by two years. It is a pity that Lockhart was not set to work chasing down those criminals responsible for the failure to archive the series. No complete episodes of *Murder Bag* survive; only 25 of 236 *No Hiding Place* episodes exist in full or partial form.

---ooo---

The American approach to crime on television was heavily influenced by *Dragnet*, starring its creator, Jack Webb. *Dragnet* began as a radio drama (1949—57). A total of 276 TV episodes followed in the 1951—59 period. There were three revivals (1967—70, 1989-91 and 2003—04). A total of 762 episodes of *Dragnet* were made (including the radio series).

Jack Webb played Sergeant Joe Friday of the Los Angeles Police Department. He starred in the radio show, the 1950s television series and the first of the revivals. There were also three *Dragnet* films. The final TV revival was broadcast after Webb's death. The *Dragnet* theme's ominous notes (*Danger ahead*) reflected Miklós Rózsa's score for the 1946 film *The Killers*. Each episode opened with the immortal lines: "Ladies and gentlemen, the story you are about to see is true. Only the names have been changed, to protect the innocent". It is hard to overstate the cultural impact of *Dragnet*. Jack Webb's goal was total realism and he was the complete perfectionist.

Millions first became aware of what police work was really like through *Dragnet*. There was the dull routine, punctuated by occasional moments of acute danger. Webb's fascination with the subject had been kindled by a modest part as a police forensic expert in the 1948 film *He Walked By Night*. The style was semi-documentary, with a former LAPD Sergeant as technical advisor. He shared stories of past cases with Webb, who then had the idea of creating a realistic radio drama based on actual crimes. Jack Webb attended Police Academy courses and accompanied night patrols, to ensure *Dragnet* was as realistic as possible.

Webb's character, Joe Friday, was a strange mix of deadpan delivery and quiet compassion. The dialogue was austere and each stage of the investigation unfolded as it did in real life. The result was entirely authentic and police officers were amongst the biggest fans. Webb's drive for accuracy knew no bounds. LAPD's actual radio call sign was used. The names of many serving police officers were used, including the Chief of Detectives. The series introduced the audience to police terminology, such as "MO" (*modus operandi*) and "APB" (*All Points Bulletin*). Standards were high from the earliest radio episodes. For example, listeners heard the exact number of footsteps it took to move from one area of LAPD headquarters to another. The radio programme also initiated the series' traditional conclusion – when the fate of the perpetrator or perpetrators was announced. Murderers were often put to death in "the lethal gas chamber at the State Penitentiary, San Quentin, California".

The radio programme broke new ground in storylines, blending the pedestrian (white collar theft or fraud, for example) with the intense drama of armed robbery, kidnap and murder. There was room for sordid cases involving pornography and prostitution. The move to television gave Webb even greater scope for realism. Set designers created exact replicas of the LAPD Robbery and Homicide Division offices. LAPD contributed, by arranging the daily loan of real LAPD badges (brought in every day by the officer acting as technical adviser). Joe Friday had a famous catchphrase when interviewing crime victims or witnesses: "Just the facts, Ma'am. Just the facts." The programme's sign-off underlined that crime doesn't pay. The criminal or criminals appeared before the camera and the court verdict and sentence were revealed. So simple... so effective.

Webb continued to introduce the names of serving police officers into his scripts, often in recognition of the assistance he received. As the first TV series neared its end, Joe Friday was promoted to Lieutenant and his partner, Frank Smith, became a Sergeant. They continued as partners, with Joe Friday retaining his famous 714 badge number. When Webb died, LAPD Chief Daryl Gates retired badge 714 and provided an LAPD Honour Guard for the funeral. Badge 714 and Webb's LAPD ID Card are now exhibited at the Los Angeles Police Academy.

An East Coast counterpart – less celebrated than *Dragnet* but excellent, nonetheless – was *The Naked City* (1958—63). It was inspired by the 1948 film of the same name. This series was anchored in New York City and told the stories of the detectives of the 65th Precinct. Criminal characters and victims provided the focus and the programmes had a high dramatic quality, appreciated by audiences and critics alike. Much of the filming took place in the South Bronx and Greenwich Village, giving the city itself a lead role. This series is best remembered for its closing line: "There are eight million stories in The Naked City. This has been one of them." A host of stars brought the stories to life, including: Rip Torn, Peter Falk, George Segal, Kim Hunter, George C. Scott, Claude Rains, Dustin Hoffman, Martin Sheen, Robert Redford and Jon Voight.

Highway Patrol (1955—59) was in a different vein. Broderick Crawford starred as Chief Dan Matthews of the California Highway Patrol. He shared the billing with a galaxy of sleek patrol cars, motorcycles and in-car police radio. The Chief's sign-off – "Ten-four!" – became a lasting catchphrase. Kids in British playgrounds ran around with their hands to their mouths, shouting "Ten-four!"

Our family went through a ritual every Saturday evening. Dad prepared for his railway night shift. In the winter, he always had a supper of *Heinz* tomato soup, sharing it with the kids. We then watched *77 Sunset Strip* (1958—64), a quirky private detective series set in Los Angeles and starring Efrem Zimbalist, Jr. as Stuart "Stu" Bailey. His partner, Jeff Spenser, was played by Roger Smith. Other characters included Roscoe, a racetrack tout, and Gerald Lloyd "Kookie" Kookson, a valet parking attendant at Dino's Restaurant, next door to the detective agency's swish offices. Kookie wanted to be a detective and his character came to dominate the series. He was something of a cultural sensation. Kookie loved Rock and Roll and he was obsessed with combing his hair. I remember combing my hair, Kookie-style, whilst walking along the street. A man working in his garden called out: "If you carry on combing it like that, it'll all fall out!" Kookie had strange catchphrases and contributed much to the series' light-hearted, "cool" style. Ambitious young actors fought for a guest slot. The winners included: Roger Moore, William Shatner, Adam West, Deforest Kelly and Mary Tyler Moore. Mature stars also appeared, including Buddy Epsen, Peter Lorre and Burgess Meredith. Even Fay Wray made an appearance!

Some American series were difficult to categorise, such as the escapist *Route 66* (1960—66), a "road drama" featuring Tod Stiles (Martin Milner), Buz Murdock (George Maharis) and a Corvette convertible. I took little interest, preferring *Sea Hunt* (1958—61), with Lloyd Bridges as scuba-diving adventurer Mike Nelson. Bridges received scuba-diving training and undertook almost all the underwater work. The underwater sequences were narrated by Bridges, who then appeared at the end with a final comment – usually a plea for more respect for the marine environment. The success of this series surprised the networks – scuba-diving was still a novelty in the 1950s. Up and coming actors appearing in *Sea Hunt* included Larry Hagman, Leonard Nimoy and Jack Nicholson. There were also parts for Lloyd Bridges' two sons, Beau and Jeff.

---oOo---

Eccentric British series included *Whack-O!* (1956—60). Jimmy Edwards starred as the drunken, less than honest Professor Jimmy Edwards M.A., Headmaster of Chiselbury, a public school for the sons of gentlefolk. The title referred to the Headmaster's enthusiasm for beating pupils with great vigour. His favourite target was the boy Wendover: "Bend over, Wendover!" Edwards' aim was true, his handlebar moustache (a legacy of wartime RAF service) twitching in satisfaction. Arthur Howard was an excellent foil as science master Oliver Pettigrew, the neurotic Assistant Headmaster. His discomfort grew as he witnessed the Professor's efforts to generate more funds for beer-drinking and gambling. As far as I was concerned, it was quite normal for Masters – especially Headmasters – to wear Mortar Boards and cane boys for minor indiscretions.

This type of school environment also provided the backdrop for *Billy Bunter*. The hapless pupil of Greyfriars School first appeared in *The Magnet* in 1908. The TV series (1952—61) starred Gerald Campion as "The fat owl of the Remove". The 40 episodes explored Bunter's flawed character – a greedy, cowardly liar who constantly failed to get his podgy hands on other chaps "tuck". His father was stingy and Bunter constantly sought loans on the back of non-existent Postal Orders. Campion was brilliant as Bunter, with his irritating "Tee, he, he" giggle, opening gambit ("I say, you fellows"), expressions such as "Oh Lor" and "Oh, crikey" and his cry of pain when kicked or beaten: "Yarooh" (hooray spelt backwards). Bunter's nemesis was the impressively-named Horace Henry Samuel Quelch, M.A., the Remove (Lower Fourth Form) Master.

My tastes in comedy, though broad, did not embrace the slapstick antics of *Mr Pastry*. Richard Hearne developed this character in a 1936 stage show, in which he appeared alongside the bulky, monocled Fred Emney (one of my Dad's favourites). *Mr Pastry* became a television star and had his own series. He appeared frequently on the BBC, with his trademark walrus moustache and bowler hat.

The Army Game (1957—61) was a firm favourite. This series followed the reluctant conscripts of a Surplus Ordnance Depot at Nether Hopping, Staffordshire. It was a huge hit with National Servicemen, their families and the public at large. It was broadcast every Friday evening and I hurried home from Cubs to watch it. The Hut 29 NCO was Michael Medwin's Eastender, Corporal Springer. His motley mates included Alfie Bass' Private "Excused Boots" Bisley, Norman Rossington's Private "Cupcake" Cook, Bernard Bresslaw's inspired Private "Popeye" Popplewell (a character not over-endowed with intelligence but with an indelible catchphrase: "I only arsked!") and Charles Hawtrey's Private "Professor" Hatchett (who found everything about the Army extremely vulgar). There were later additions, including

Harry Fowler's Corporal "Flogger" Hoskins and Dick Emery's Private "Chubby" Catchpole.

The officers were also amusing, including Geoffrey Sumner's Major Upshot-Bagley and Frank Williams' Captain Pocket. My favourite character, by far, was William Hartnell's permanently frustrated and aptly named Sergeant-Major Bullimore. I have not forgotten his cry of rage: "Well... I never did in all my life!" He was succeeded by Bill Fraser, as Sergeant-Major Snudge – who later teamed up with Alfie Bass in the series *Bootsie and Snudge* (1960—63).

---ooo---

I did not rush home for the quiz show *Double Your Money* (1955—68), hosted by "most sincerely, folks" Hughie Green. One contestant on the show would progress to the £1,000 "Treasure Trail" and its sound-proof "Isolation Booth". *Double Your Money* began on Radio Luxembourg and moved to television when commercial broadcasting began in Britain. Green was a very successful presenter of game shows and went on to host *The Sky's the Limit* and *Opportunity Knocks*. His shows always left me cold. I felt the same way about *Take your pick* (1955—68), hosted by Michael Miles (later, Des O'Connor, in the 1992—98 revival). This show also originated on Radio Luxembourg and featured the intensely irritating "Yes-No Interlude". Contestants had to answer rapid-fire questions without using "yes" or "no".

Wildlife programmes held more interest, especially the adventures of *Armand and Michaela Denis*. Armand was a Belgian adventurer who specialised in making documentaries in remote parts of the world. Michaela married Armand in Bolivia in 1948. They went to Africa to work on the film *King Solomon's Mines* (Michaela acted as Deborah Kerr's double). They went on to become BBC Television stalwarts; Armand produced marvellous films and Michaela provided "glam".

Zoo Time (1956—68) was another staple. It was hosted by Desmond Morris, who later wrote *The Naked Ape*. This was the first natural history series for children and was not without drama. The live TV escapees included a cobra and a vampire bat. There was also the episode when a lion mounted a lioness. Desmond Morris moved on briskly but the next lion promptly did the same thing! My most vivid memory of *Zoo Time* is Desmond Morris holding a chimp, its hands exploring the human face with friendly and gentle curiosity.

The best wildlife series of all, however, featured the undersea adventures of *Hans and Lotte Hass*. Hans was a Frogman during World War Two. Subsequently, he resumed his career as a zoologist, diver and film-maker. There were expeditions to the Red Sea and East Africa. He married Lotte in 1950. Hans Hass was the first man to film mantas and whale sharks underwater.

---ooo---

Some early 1950s TV programmes have left just dim memories. One such was *The Appleyards*, an early soap for children based around Mr and Mrs Appleyard and their four children: teenagers Janet and John and the younger Margaret and Tommy. This programme specialised in trivia. All I can remember is the programme name. *The Appleyards* was a junior version of *The Grove Family* (1954—57). This TV soap – the first of its kind – told the story of a "typical" middle class family. Written by the father and elder brother of Jon Pertwee, it attracted a huge audience (including, apparently, the Queen Mother). Once again, I remember little, other than Nancy Roberts as the miserable, poisonous "Granny Grove".

Other dim memories include the beautiful Australian singer Shirley Abicair, who played the zither, and the stunning singer Yana – a frequent guest on variety shows. Even at the tender age of nine or ten, I wondered how anyone could actually fit into a dress that tight.

My tastes began to develop. I was fascinated by "mystery" and the complexities of human behaviour. I relished *Alfred Hitchcock presents*, with its wonderful opening: a cartoon of the great man's distinctive profile, a curious, bumbling theme (*Funeral march of a marionette*), Hitchcock's walk-on and that curiously flat greeting: "Good evening!" This series was packed with stars, from Bette Davis, Jayne Mansfield, Angie Dickinson and Diana Dors to Gene Barry, Christopher Lee, Walter Matthau, Vincent Price and Robert Redford.

For my money, the most intriguing programme of all was *The Human Jungle*, a later series (1963—64). It starred Herbert Lom as consulting psychiatrist Dr Roger Corder. He had a Harley Street practice and also saw patients at a local hospital. I was mesmerised by the phobias and irrationalities of Corder's patients and, even more, by the tactics he employed when treating them. Guest stars included Margaret Lockwood, Rita Tushingham, Flora Robson and Roger Livesey.

---ooo---

Westerns were under threat of extinction by the late 1960s. Dull-witted "parental advocacy groups" argued that Westerns were too violent for children. They should have saved their ammunition for the super-violent video games of today. The two surviving Western series, *Gunsmoke* and *Bonanza*, ended in the mid-1970s.

Robin Hood, Arthur, Hereward the Wake and other heroic figures of Britain's past continue to interest me. The ideals of justice and freedom from a life of subjugation resonate strongly in today's world. Was Robin Hood real? The answer, in all probability, is yes – many times over (although I doubt whether many (if any) real Robin Hoods robbed the rich to give to the poor). What evidence exists for a real Robin includes references to the long established Hode family in the historical heartland of the legend, Barnsdale in Yorkshire. If Robin Hood was real, he was almost certainly a Yeoman, rather than a nobleman, and he lived his outlaw life as a matter of necessity.

William Russell (or Sir Lancelot, as I knew him) moved on to *Dr Who* and became one of the Good Doctor's travelling companions. I was more startled, in later life, to see Sir Lancelot turn up in *Coronation Street*. He was without horse, shield, plumed helmet and lance! Perhaps these are not essential in "Weatherfield".

Episodes of Rod Serling's original *The Twilight Zone* hold up well today. I much enjoyed the 1983 *Twilight Zone* movie and was most impressed with John Landis' prologue – a truck driver and passenger travelling at night on a lonely road and recalling TV themes of yesteryear – including, of course, *The Twilight Zone*. Then comes that fateful question: "Would you like to see something really scary?" If you, the reader, are ever asked this question, the correct answer is: "No!"

The outer limits was revived over the 1995–2002 period. As in the past, it was biased towards science fiction rather than fantasy. The traditional dramatic plot twist was maintained. There was less emphasis on "Monster of the Week", but there was no shortage of aliens threatening destruction. The *Control Voice* on the revived show's DVD release has moved with the times: "There is nothing wrong with your DVD player... etc... etc."

As for those scary early science fiction programmes, I happened to be flicking through channels recently when I suddenly found *The Trollenberg Terror*. I had to watch it. I was amazed at its tame plot, the formal 1950s evening dresses of the ladies (rather out of place, even then, in a mountain resort) and, most of all, the spectacle of Warren Mitchell playing "Professor Crevett". *A for Andromeda* was remade by the BBC in 2006 but fell flat. It seemed old hat. People no longer needed to be reminded that DNA really exists!

Modern American crime series fail to satisfy. Few stand out in terms of dramatic quality. *Hill Street Blues* was special and *NYPD Blue* ranks among the best. There is also something about Jerry Orbach's Lennie Briscoe character, in

Law and Order, that connects to the glory days of *Dragnet* and Joe Friday. The rest have little impact, being a succession of glossy CSI-type clones. Everything, from police proceedings and forensic science to human emotion, is ruthlessly exploited for maximum "audience hook". Unfortunately, they tend to achieve exactly the opposite, at least in my case.

Meanwhile, the great names of my television past have gradually slipped away. *Mr Pastry*, Richard Hearne, died in 1971. Armand Denis also died in 1971, although Michaela lived on for over 30 years, becoming a spiritual healer and, subsequently, a property developer. She died in Nairobi in 2003, at the age of 88. Another beautiful woman, Yana, died at the early age of 62 in the late 1980s, her passing largely unnoticed.

---ooo---

– 12 –

Red Plush and Choc-Ices

I knew three cinemas as a child. The nearest, just around the corner, was the Lee Green *Savoy*. This tiny cinema was convenient and cosy. The others were in Lewisham: the *Gaumont Palace*, resplendent in red plush and seating around 3,000, and the more modest *Rex*. The *Gaumont* (later the *Odeon*), really was a palace. It opened in 1932 and was vast and lavishly decorated. The Rex, more downmarket, was situated next to the railway and the picture shuddered when trains passed.

People were accustomed to queuing for a popular film. "Going to the pictures", or "the flicks", was an escape into another world, made more mysterious by the towering swirls of cigarette smoke caught in the projectionist's beam. Choc-ices, tubs and *Kia-Ora* orange drinks were available from the ice-cream lady's tray. Her hand-torch illuminated the goodies. The cinema gave value for money, with a main feature, a "B film" and Pearl & Dean's advertising.

Competitive pressure from television prompted some lavish 1950s epics, such as The *Ten Commandments* (1956) and *Ben Hur* (1959). Westerns and war were main themes, but there was also Cold War paranoia, fear of the atomic bomb and the UFO craze. This led to science fiction classics such as *When Worlds Collide* and *The Day the Earth Stood Still*, both released in 1951, together with later productions such as *The War of the Worlds* (1953), *This Island Earth* (1955), *Forbidden Planet* (1956) and *Them* (1954). There was also a peculiarly effective horror film, which conveyed real terror by suggestion, rather than special effects trickery. This was the creepy 1957 release *Night of the Demon*.

Westerns were dominated by John Wayne, James Stewart and Henry Fonda. Outstanding Westerns included John Ford's cavalry trilogy and *The Searchers*, a remarkably gritty production for its time. Alfred Hitchcock was the master of "mystery and suspense". His achievements included *Strangers on a Train* (1951), *Rear Window* (1954), *Vertigo* (1958) and *North by Northwest* (1959).

Notable films of this period included *King Solomon's Mines* (1950), *African Queen* (1951), *High Noon* (1952) and *The Man from Laramie* (1955). The huge hit of 1955 was *Davy Crockett, king of the wild frontier*, with a popular song beginning: "Born on a mountaintop in Tennessee..." I was crazy about Davy Crockett and was one of countless thousands who forced their mothers to buy them Davy Crockett hats. It should have been made of racoon fur but my one was almost certainly rabbit. I insisted on wearing that fur hat, with its long hanging "tail", at all times... even in bed.

Westerns were popular but 1950s British cinema was dominated by war films. The Royal Navy was represented by *The Battle of the River Plate* (1959), with its terrifying representation of a "big gun" naval battle. The Battle of the Atlantic had been portrayed in *The Cruel Sea* (1953). Royal Air Force tributes included *The Dam Busters* (1955) and *Reach for the Sky* (1956). As for the Army, the outstanding films included *The Bridge on the River Kwai* (1957) and 1958 releases *Dunkirk*, *Ice Cold in Alex* and *I was Monty's Double*. By the age of eleven I had reached the obvious conclusion: John Mills, Jack Hawkins and Richard Todd had been largely responsible for Hitler's demise.

---ooo---

Cinema audiences fell sharply in the 1950s (from 1.37 billion admissions in 1951 to 500 million in 1960), reflecting the growth of the television audience. Yet the 1950s produced some remarkable films. War was a subject still fresh in the public mind. The physical evidence of war was all around, with bombsites and peeling signs on walls pointing the way to the nearest shelter. Westerns, on the other hand, were an escape into a different world. To my recollection, no 1950s boy *wanted* to be an "Indian". Indians were "baddies", although some Westerns were beginning to portray Native Americans in a more sympathetic light. One film, for example, recognised a mounted force of Indians as "the finest light cavalry in the world". I had my toy six-gun and a supply of explosive caps, but I also kept a bow and arrow in reserve, just in case.

We stayed up on Saturday evenings to watch the film. This ended badly on one occasion, when *They Died With Their Boots On* (1941) was screened. This inaccurate account of George Armstrong Custer's life ends with his command encircled at the Little Big Horn. The opposition included Anthony Quinn, as Crazy Horse. My five-year-old brother, Colin, was unfamiliar with the story and refused to accept that Custer had died. As Errol Flynn fell, Colin turned red and burst into tears. He couldn't stand "Custer's Last Stand". Warner Brothers, however, shed no tears. This film grossed USD 2.55 million and was the studio's second biggest hit in 1941. Apparently, only 16 extras were Sioux Indians; the rest were Filipinos. This film made much use of the stirring *Garry Owen* – said to have been Custer's favourite tune. Adults and kids whistled a lot in the 1950s; I often whistled *Garry Owen* as I walked.

John Wayne was the ultimate Western hero. With his unmistakable voice, huge frame and total self-belief, "The Duke" first rose to prominence in *Stagecoach* (1939). He continued to play essentially the same character until his last film, *The Shootist* (1976), when he portrayed an aging gunfighter dying of cancer. This disease took his life just a few years later.

My favourite John Wayne film is the second in John Ford's trilogy. *She Wore a Yellow Ribbon* (1949) is set immediately after the Little Big Horn massacre. John Wayne is Captain Nathan Brittles, briefed for one last mission before retiring from the Cavalry. Victor McLaglen is the perfect foil to Wayne – known to him as "Captain, Darling!" He plays the hard-drinking Top Sergeant Quincannon. The fight scene featuring Quincannon is unforgettable, as is Wayne's visit to the Indian encampment and his conversation with the old chief: "Naaathon... my friend!" His toothless counterpart, Chief Pony That Walks, is played with gusto by Chief John Big Tree. The music is memorable – the marching song *She Wore a Yellow Ribbon* – as is the fantastic vista of The Mittens, Monument Valley's most dramatic feature. What a film!

---ooo---

War films, especially British war films, made a big impact. At one level, they had great simplicity: everything British was good and everything about Nazi Germany was very bad. One side stood for civilisation and freedom. The other represented barbarism and the dark side. The war had finished barely a decade before and right had triumphed over might. The actors and actresses starring in these films were of their time; they had a stamp of authenticity which is beyond reach today.

Early British war films with a documentary feel included *The Lion Has Wings* (1939) and *Target for Tonight* (1941). The latter starred a serving Wellington bomber crew. The "Skipper" was Wing Commander Pickard – an outstanding operational pilot, who died later during a low-level Mosquito attack to free resistance fighters from Amiens Prison. The early war films had a mixed reception but later productions skilfully blended documentary technique and fiction. Notable examples included *In Which We Serve* (1942) and *The Way Ahead* (1944).

Wartime releases included the American productions *Mrs Miniver* (1942) and *Guadalcanal Diary* (1943). Post-war British releases included *The Dam Busters*, *Reach For The Sky* and *Sink the Bismarck* (1960). Worthy American post-war offerings included John Wayne's *Sands of Iwo Jima* (1949) and *Halls of Montezuma* (1950). There were also outstanding prisoner of war films, such as *The wooden horse* (1950) and *The Colditz story* (1955).

---ooo---

Mrs Miniver was an almost laughable American attempt to portray a "typical" English household. It assumed that most middle class families had large houses and gardens with a private jetty on the Thames. At another level, however, this film was a masterstroke. It made a significant contribution to the task of boosting American public support for the British, in their struggle to the death against Nazism. The film's strengths included an absorbing plot, strong characterisation and the stunning Greer Garson as Mrs Miniver. Walter Pidgeon played her husband. My Mum described *Mrs Miniver,* the winner of six Academy Awards, as the best "weepie" ever. It was the top box office attraction of 1942 and the second biggest film of the 1940s – beaten only by *Gone With The Wind*. The film ends in a stirring oration, given in a bombed, roofless church as a flight of RAF fighters pass overhead. It concludes with the words: "And may God defend the right".

Richard Ney played Greer Garson's eldest son, "Vin". They fell in love during the filming and married soon after, despite an 11-year age gap. Greer Garson went on to make the longest ever "Best Actress" *Oscar* acceptance speech. It lasted five and a half minutes, prompting the introduction of a limit for all future speeches. As a young boy I was jealous of "Vin". Greer Garson was my first experience of love at first sight. I felt it was very selfish of her to "die" several years later, in *The Miniver Story* (1950) – another outstanding weepie for Mum. Vin, the eldest son in the earlier film, made no appearance in the sequel, possibly because Richard Ney and Greer Garson had divorced by that time.

---ooo---

The outstanding 1950s war film was *The Dam Busters*. This story, so utterly BRITISH, has vivid portrayals of Barnes Wallis and Guy Gibson. The stars also include the aircraft: several Lancasters were brought out of storage for the filming. Apparently, they cost £130 an hour to operate and the flying bill amounted to 10 per cent of total film production costs. This understated epic is a tale of three challenges: the struggle to persuade the "Upkeep" bouncing bomb to work, the challenge of winning acceptance of Wallis' proposals to attack the great Ruhr dams and, finally, the supreme test: delivering the bouncing bombs (more properly, mines) hard against the dam walls. The film's only weakness, to my mind, is the rather clumsy representation of the explosions, but this is as nothing when set against the film's masterly qualities and Eric Coates' stirring *Dam Busters' March*.

Michael Redgrave and Richard Todd are both effective in their roles. Todd, in particular, has a convincing manner that, perhaps, draws on his own wartime experience. This film comes alive in the air. The flying sequences have never been bettered, especially the low flying over reservoirs and dams in England. The closing scene is an impressive example of restraint, with Todd's Gibson taking his leave of the distraught scientist with the quiet comment that he has letters to write. These are letters that the real Gibson had to write to the families of the eight missing crews. Fifty-six men did not return (53 of whom died). This film's many highlights include the heartfelt comment by an Australian bomb-aimer, as his aircraft practised flying over water at 60 ft at night: "This is bloody dangerous!"

In later years Barnes Wallis made it clear that there had been no significant bureaucratic opposition to the Dams attack. The film-makers had indulged in dramatic licence. The same can be said of the suggestion that it was Gibson's idea to maintain the correct height by using spotlights (portrayed as a revelation during an evening at the theatre). The bouncing bomb was still secret in the early 1950s (despite the fact that the Germans had recovered an intact specimen from one of the crashed Lancasters, back in 1943). The film shows the weapon as spherical, rather than cylindrical.

Watching *The Dam Busters* as a young boy had consequences. Firstly, I finally persuaded my parents to part with 7/6d, to buy an Airfix Lancaster model. I put this together with Dad's help (I don't know who enjoyed it more). Secondly, the film planted the seeds of my lifelong interest in the Air Force. Much later in life, it encouraged me to write a book (*Life and Death in Bomber Command*). I have also taken part in two Bomber Command battlefield tours (one visiting bases and former bases in the UK, including Scampton, and the second involving a tour of the targets). The Mohne Dam is impressive: the huge breach in its walls is clearly visible – the "fresh" brickwork is quite distinct.

Prior to *The Dam Busters*, the Lancasters used in that film had roles in an earlier, less well known production, *Appointment in London* (1953). Dirk Bogarde plays a squadron commander close to breaking point. This film closely parallels an American equivalent, *Twelve O' clock High* (with Gregory Peck pushed to the limit by command pressures and the steady attrition of daylight bombing).

Dirk Bogarde's performance has a stark realism. The taut, brooding atmosphere conveys the unrelenting strain that must have been felt in the billets and mess when losses were severe. The film shows the camaraderie and some rather forced partying by those drinking to forget. The bombing raid at the film's climax is extraordinary. Yet, perhaps the best scene is a low-key conversation between Bogarde's Wing Commander Tim Mason and Sam Kydd, playing Ackroyd – a lowly airman with a ground job. This takes place in a deserted hangar and their exchanges are softly spoken and entirely natural.

Mason, with 87 sorties in his logbook, is determined to complete 90 trips. Although told he is to be rested, he staggers on until grounded for his own good. Nevertheless, circumstances allow him to make that final operation. He survives and is lucky enough to win the heart of the ravishing Dinah Sheridan – who plays widowed Wren Eve Canyon. The film's title refers to Mason's attendance at Buckingham Palace, to be decorated by King George Vl.

The authenticity of *Appointment in London* is due in part to the involvement of composer John Wooldridge, who co-wrote the screenplay. Wooldridge drew on his immense experience as an operational bomber pilot – he completed more sorties than the film's fictitious Wing Commander.

RAF Fighter Command also had a film presence in the 1950s. Perhaps the outstanding example is *Reach for the Sky*, released just 16 years after the Battle of Britain. This is a kindly biopic of legless fighter ace Douglas Bader, a man with extreme reservoirs of courage. Kenneth More plays Bader and is as believable as Richard Todd's Guy Gibson. On More's arm is the lovely Muriel Pavlow as Thelma Bader. This film is a product of its time; the characters are convincing and the plot is gripping. Bader was an enthusiastic cricket and rugby player who foolishly rose to a challenge at a flying club. He crashed during low-flying aerobatics and both legs were amputated. Fitted with "tin legs", he fought for acceptance as a fighter pilot on the eve of war with Germany. Overcoming all opposition, he began flying operationally but was eventually lost over France. He was taken prisoner and immediately began making life miserable for his captors. When eventually freed, his aircraft headed the huge victory flypast over London in September 1945.

This film has many memorable sequences. Perhaps the most moving deal with Bader's early attempts to walk with artificial legs. More's portrayal of the raw agony is unforgettable. *Reach for the Sky* won the BAFTA Award for the Best British Film of 1956.

---oOo---

The war at sea also received attention. One great film was *The Sea Shall Not Have Them* (1954), starring Michael Redgrave, Dirk Bogarde and Anthony Steel. The title is the motto of the RAF's Air Sea Rescue Service. The film portrays efforts to locate the dinghy from an RAF aircraft forced to ditch in the North Sea. The Air Sea Rescue launch triumphs after many setbacks, including bad weather, engine trouble and a galley fire. I enjoyed this film so much that my Christmas presents included a wonderful clockwork Air Sea Rescue launch. It performed well in our long tin bath, despite the lack of dinghies.

Perhaps the definitive film portrayal of the Navy's war was *The Cruel Sea*, based on Nicholas Monsarrat's best seller about the Battle of the Atlantic and the struggle to overcome Germany's U-boats. Jack Hawkins plays Ericson, Captain of the corvette *Compass Rose*. This film conveys the crushing fatigue, cold and desperate boredom of convoy protection. It also illustrates the horrifying choices that could confront a commander at any time. Ericson decides to drop depth charges on a U-boat, despite the fact that the explosions will kill survivors in the water. He then tries (and fails) to drown his sorrows. Later, *Compass Rose* is sunk and Hawkins and his survivors man the new frigate *Saltash Castle*. Two submarines are sunk, one credited to each vessel. The film opens with Hawkins' moving voice-over: "This is a story of the Battle of the Atlantic. The story of an ocean, two ships and a handful of men. The men are the heroes. The heroines are the ships. The only villain is the sea, the cruel sea, that man has made more cruel..." With this rousing opening and Jack Hawkins' very special voice, how could the film fail?

Run Silent, Run Deep (1958) also made a big impression. Dad took me to see it at Lee Green's *Savoy* cinema. The film explores the tensions of submarine warfare and the conflict between Clark Gable, who plays Commander Richardson, and Burt Lancaster, who plays his second in command. Their rivalry reaches a climax as Richardson ignores orders and sets out to sink the Japanese destroyer that attacked his previous command, regardless of the risks to his new crew. Both men put in fine performances, with the claustrophobia heightened by filming aboard a real submarine. This film has a special claim to fame, in that it was premiered underwater, on board the *USS Perch*.

---ooo---

Some war films focused on the raw heroism of individuals, such as Sergeant Major Charles Coward, portrayed in *The Password is Courage* (1962). The actual password was the more prosaic "cleaning cloths". Another example was *Carve Her Name*

With Pride (1958), the story of SOE operative Violet Szabo, captured and killed by the Nazis. Virginia McKenna gave an excellent performance as the George Cross heroine. Later, I discovered that this film shied away from the extreme brutality meted out to her in Ravensbrück concentration camp. Szabo's beauty was matched by that of Virginia McKenna, who was convincing as the former shop assistant who wanted to kill Germans to avenge her French husband, killed on war service.

The Cockleshell Heroes (1955) told the story of *Operation Frankton*, the commando raid on shipping at Bordeaux. It was carried out by five small canoes carrying 10 very brave men who had been briefed to place limpet mines. The film's cast included Trevor Howard and Anthony Newley. Only two of the Royal Marines survived the December 1942 attack. Two others capsized and died of hypothermia. Six were captured and murdered by the Germans. The limpet mines damaged six ships.

Some 1950s war films tell unlikely stories that are founded in fact. *The Wooden Horse* (1950) tells of an amazing escape plan. The prisoners' huts were sited a long way from the perimeter wire, making tunnelling difficult. The ingenious solution (thought up by Flight Lieutenant Eric Williams and a fellow prisoner) involved placing a vaulting horse near the wire. A PT group practiced vaulting every day, whilst the man hidden inside the horse dug a tunnel under the perimeter of Stalag Luft lll, Sagan. All signs of the tunnel entrance were disguised before the horse was put away after PT. Three men escaped by this means, after 114 days of digging and vaulting. They reached Sweden and were eventually repatriated to the UK. One camp vaulter was the actor Peter Butterworth, a popular Children's Television figure of the 1950s.

I Was Monty's Double (1958) was even more unlikely. It starred M.E. Clifton-James, *who was Monty's double!* During the war he impersonated the General to fool the Germans. Not surprisingly, Clifton-James was a "natural" in this role, playing alongside John Mills and Michael Hordern. During the war Clifton-James, an actor, had served in the Pay Corps. His remarkable resemblance to Monty led to an overnight promotion to "General". His job was to convince the Germans that Montgomery was on tour, with no major operation pending. There was some dramatic licence, as the film includes an attempt to kidnap Monty that has no foundation in fact. The Intelligence Officer who recruited Clifton-James for his real mission during the war knew something about acting; he was none other than David Niven.

Without doubt, the strangest story of all was *The Man Who Never Was* (1956), from the book of the same name published three years earlier by Lieutenant

Commander Ewen Montagu, responsible for the deception known as *Operation Mincemeat*. The idea was to convince the Germans that the Allies planned to invade Greece and Sardinia in 1943, rather than the more obvious Sicily. Documents were planted on a body, revealing the false Greece/Sardinia plan. The corpse – presented as the victim of an air crash – was released by submarine and drifted onto the Spanish coast. The pro-Axis authorities gave the Germans access to the "find".

The body was released by *HMS Seraph* on 30 April, off the Spanish town of Huelva, and it was found the next morning by a local fisherman. "Major Martin" was buried with full military honours on 4 May and his loss was recorded by *The Times* of 4 June. When the briefcase was returned, it was found that the documents had been opened. Hitler was convinced and ordered reinforcements to Greece, Sardinia and Corsica. On 9 July the Allies landed on Sicily. I was mesmerised by the complexities of the plot.

Where did Montagu get that body? A debate has rumbled on over the decades. Montagu never revealed the identity. In 1996 it was claimed that "Major Martin" was, in fact, a Welsh alcoholic who died after ingesting rat poison. This man, Glyndwr Michael, died at a London hospital on 28 January, 1943. Martin's gravestone at Huelva Cemetery was subsequently inscribed: "Glyndwr Michael served as Major William Martin". An alternative solution then emerged – the claim that the body was that of a drowned sailor from the escort carrier *HMS Dasher*, lost off the Scottish coast in late March 1943. The confusion was compounded when rival claims named two different members of *HMS Dasher's* crew! The Naval Historical Branch still insists that the body was that of Glyndwr Michael. Mystery continues to surround *Operation Mincemeat*. Did Montagu acquire a body, or did he pinch one?

---ooo---

Such cloak and dagger tactics had no place in John Wayne's cinematic war. His films included *Sands of Iwo Jima*. "The Duke" played Marine Sergeant John Stryker, who is killed by a sniper – to the great distress of myself and my younger brother, Colin. British war films were deeper and more complex. One outstanding example is David Lean's *The Bridge On The River Kwai*, starring Jack Hawkins, William Holden and Alec Guinness (as Lieutenant Colonel Nicholson). Prisoners are put to work building a railway bridge for the Japanese. Nicholson makes every effort to see that the bridge is constructed as quickly as possible, having decided that the project's boost to morale outweighs its military value to the Japanese.

A commando team is dispatched to destroy the bridge upon completion. Many years later, I learnt that the senior British officer involved was, in fact, Lieutenant Colonel Philip Toosey – who did everything he could to *slow* the building of the bridge. Nevertheless, the film won seven Oscars.

---ooo---

General adventure films made little impression on me. I enjoyed Stewart Grainger's Allan Quatermain in *King Solomon's Mines* (1950), based on H. Rider Haggard's 1885 novel. *The Four Feathers* (1939), starring John Clements and Ralph Richardson, made a bigger impact. This concerned Kitchener's war against the Dervishes. Clements plays Lieutenant Harry Faversham, who resigns his commission before the campaign and is then accused of cowardice. His friends send him white feathers. Subsequently, he becomes a hero when, disguised as a native, he works to save his friends and return the white feathers. A "ripping yarn"!

Some comedies amused me. I enjoyed William Hartnell's Sergeant Major in *Carry on Sergeant* (1958) – the very first of the "Carry on" series. Kenneth Williams, Hattie Jacques, Charles Hawtrey and Kenneth Connor were soon established as "Carry on" stalwarts.

The Blue Lamp (1950) was very British and set the scene for the popular *Dixon of Dock Green* television series. Jack Warner played the old-fashioned Copper George Dixon (despite having been killed off in the film by a youthful Dirk Bogarde). Warner was over 80 when *Dixon of Dock Green* eventually finished in 1976.

On a rainy Sunday afternoon I was cajoled into watching Mum's favourite weepie, *Random Harvest* (1942). I didn't really mind, as it starred the delicious Greer Garson, of *Mrs Miniver* fame. Ronald Colman played the shell-shocked Great War soldier known as "John Smith", who had lost his memory. He falls in love with Garson, as showgirl Paula. They marry but "Smithy" is run over on his way to a job interview and his memory returns. He is the very wealthy Charles Rainier, now left with no recollection of his life with Paula. As the years pass he becomes increasingly successful as an industrialist. Paula sees his photograph in a newspaper and joins him as his secretary (her marriage having been dissolved, with Smith declared legally dead). Charles becomes an MP, supported by Paula (now known as Margaret). He then proposes to her on a businesslike, rather than romantic basis. Eventually, of course, his memory returns, with my Mum in floods of tears. I had no tears. I was too much in love with Greer Garson.

The actress, a major MGM star, was born in Essex in 1904. Greer Garson died in 1996 in Dallas, Texas. Her porcelain beauty was matched by great intelligence; she had degrees in French and 18th-century literature. Garson signed with MGM in 1937 and her first film was *Goodbye, Mr Chips*. She married three times, the last to Texan oilman Buddy Fogelson. The couple lived at Forked Lightning Ranch, New Mexico. What a wonderful woman!

---ooo---

Without doubt, the weirdest film I saw as a child was *Four-sided Triangle* (1953), a British science fiction film from Hammer. Two friends build a "Reproducer". This made duplicates of anything, including the beautiful Lena – whom they both love. The solution is obvious and the unsuccessful suitor creates Helen, a duplicate of Lena. Unfortunately, *both* women love the rival. The two men now have an extra problem. I liked the idea of the Reproducer and wondered whether it might work on pocket money. I also loved the laboratory scenes, jam-packed with all sorts of flashing lights, strange gadgets and instruments.

There was also that strange cult science fiction film *The Man From Planet X* (1951). Skilful filming gave this alien an unworldly quality (nearly, but not quite, human). The being's landing coincided with a rogue planet's close approach to Earth. Given the film's shoestring budget the results were extremely effective – very scary!

---ooo---

Lewisham's *Rex Cinema* eventually became *Studios 6/7* but this change of name failed to prevent its demolition in 1988. I now find it difficult to identify the site, despite the presence of the railway line. The Lewisham *Odeon* went the same way. It closed in 1981 and was demolished 10 years later. Lee Green's *Savoy*, which had opened in 1913 as the *Imperial Picture Theatre*, closed in 1959 and was demolished in 1986. It made way for a Sainsbury's store. This disgraceful development carved the heart out of Lee Green and, in my view, is the architectural and social equivalent of a war crime.

Some things haven't changed. For example, Pearl & Dean has clocked up 60 years of cinema advertising. What is missing today, of course, is CHOICE. There is little point in looking at cinema programmes; what is shown in one is shown in all the others.

I still love black and white films. I appreciate the master's hand in Alfred Hitchcock's work. There is also the complex genius of Nick Roeg. His films, including *Don't Look Now* (1973) and *Bad Timing* (1980), have a curious presence at every viewing. I developed a taste for Andrzej Wadja's trilogy: *A Generation* (1954), *Kanal* (1956) and *Ashes and Diamonds* (1958). This Polish film-maker's father was murdered by the Soviets in the Katyn massacre. Two years later, Wadja joined the resistance. His later films include *Man of Marble* (1976) and *Man of Iron* (1981), both concerned with the long Polish struggle for freedom. In the latter, Solidarity Leader Lech Walesa appears as himself. Above all, I came to appreciate the slow, unfolding beauty of Russian Director Andrei Tarkovsky's film of Stanislaw Lem's *Solaris* (1972). The idea of an alien lifeform with the ability to "conjure up" the dead left a deep, lasting impression. What if...?

It took me years to catch up with some important films of the 1950s, including *Shane* (1953), *High Society* (1956), *Look Back in Anger* (1958) and that gripping evocation of the Titanic's loss, *A Night to Remember* (1958). With hindsight, however, my vote for the most impressive film of the 1950s goes to *Detective Story* (1951). This was brutal reality, delivered with passion by Kirk Douglas at his very best. It provided the template for countless American crime movies and series.

Westerns fell out of fashion. Beyond *Lonesome Dove*, few modern productions cut the mustard. Computer wizardry and gratuitous violence are poor substitutes for a plot. Less is more and it is usually a mistake to show everything. Today's film-makers should revisit *The Searchers* and study John Wayne's response when asked what the Indians had done to a girl captive. There was no need to show the body. "The Duke" said: "Don't ever ask me that question again!"

Today, I enjoy John Ford's westerns as much for their spectacular panoramas as the action and John Wayne's laconic drawl. Monument Valley provided a canvas like no other. John Wayne died on 11 June, 1979. He was 72. He had been unable to serve in the military in World War Two due to his age and the determination of Republic Studios to retain him. This may explain his extreme patriotism after the war. As a conservative Republican, he supported the Vietnam War. Wayne was awarded the *Congressional Gold Medal* just before his death. Later, he was awarded a posthumous *Presidential Medal of Freedom* by Jimmy Carter. It is said that the script for his last film, *The Shootist*, required him to shoot a man in the back. He refused to do it, saying: "I've made over 250 pictures and have never shot a guy in the back. Change it." *Stagecoach* is the enduring masterpiece – the perfect antidote to a rainy Sunday. As for Davy Crockett, in the shape of Fess

Parker, the actor put aside that trusty long rifle and racoon-skin cap. He became a successful property developer, hotel owner and wine-maker.

During the 1980s I renewed my acquaintance with war films of the 1940s and 1950s. I had forgotten some outstanding examples, such as *Ill Met by Moonlight* (1956) and *The Password is Courage*, both starring Dirk Bogarde. In the latter, Bogarde played the inappropriately named Sergeant-Major Coward. More recently, I learnt more of the grim reality behind Coward's incredible heroism whilst attempting to save the lives of death camp inmates. I was disappointed to find that the film had trivialised this man's terrible experiences (so terrible, in fact, that no-one believed him when he returned to Britain).

Eventually, justice found Charlie Coward. He was among 27 men and women recognised as *Heroes of the Holocaust* by the British Government in March 2010. Solid silver medals were inscribed: "In service of humanity". The medals were awarded to two survivors and 25 families, including the family of Charlie Coward. The Sergeant-Major had been captured in 1940 during the Battle of France. After several escape attempts he was sent to Auschwitz lll (Monowitz) slave labour camp, where he became Red Cross Liaison Officer for 1,400 British prisoners. He bribed an SS Guard with Swiss chocolate and, in return, was given access to the dead bodies of prisoners. He swapped the identities of dead French and Belgian slave labourers with those of Jews who were being worked to death. They were then smuggled out of the camp. He was instrumental in saving 400 lives. Coward died of cancer in 1976. He had already been recognised by Israel, being named as *Righteous Amongst Nations*. His medal was received at 10 Downing Street by his daughter. His former house, in Edmonton, now displays an English Heritage Blue Plaque. It is a pity that no film-maker has taken up Charlie Coward's true story.

---ooo---

There were few war films of any quality in the 1960s and 1970s. The exceptions included the *Battle of Britain* (1969), *Tora! Tora! Tora!* (1970) and *A Bridge Too Far* (1977). All suffered from a surfeit of big stars. In the *Battle of Britain*, make-up artists failed to create a convincing 1940s look for Susannah York's WAAF Section Officer. Somehow, despite their best efforts, she still looks like a "Swinging Sixties" girl dressed up in an old uniform. The film's aerial combat scenes are unlikely to be surpassed (if one ignores the unsuccessful Stuka models).

Much of the Spanish Air Force (still flying Rolls Royce Merlin-engined variants of Luftwaffe BF109 fighters and Heinkel 111 bombers during the 1960s) was mustered for this film. I had a remarkable experience during its production. Standing on the platform at Erith station, waiting for my London train, I heard a faint hum in the sky and noticed that many elderly commuters were looking up, rather anxiously. The drone of engines increased as a Heinkel 111 bomber flew along the Thames, representing the attack made by hundreds of similar aircraft just 29 years before. High above, a Spitfire wheeled and dived on the "raider". To one side, the camera plane held station. Whenever I watch the film sequence of this daylight attack on the capital, I realise that, 12,000 ft below, my face was amongst many thousands looking skywards.

I had enough sense in my late teens to recognise that films such as *The Dirty Dozen* (1967) and *Where Eagles Dare* (1968) were merely low grade action movies. Later, I had no time for the "neo-realism" of Vietnam War films, such as *Apocalypse Now* (1979), *Full Metal Jacket* (1987) and the Oliver Stone trilogy: *Platoon* (1986), *Born on the Fourth of July* (1989) and *Heaven & Earth* (1993). Later war films also failed to move me. Spielberg's *Saving Private Ryan* (1998) seemed to exploit the horror of the Omaha Beach landings. *Schindler's List* (1993) made compelling, bleak viewing but was spoilt by its sentimental conclusion, out of keeping when set against the sheer enormity of the crimes. Nonetheless, a later effort was as profound as any 1950s war film. *Band of Brothers* (2001), another Spielberg production, was a remarkable achievement. Wolfgang Petersen's *Das Boot* (1981) was also memorable for intensity and conviction.

Films such as *The Longest Day* (1962) and the later *A Bridge Too Far* were spectacular but over-stuffed with big names. Much harder to bear is a plan to remake *The Dam Busters*. Apparently, Guy Gibson's dog, Nigger, is to be renamed "Digger". I have seen TV screenings of the original film with the word "Nigger" bleeped out, or with a dubbed in "Trigger". I find it hard to believe that Gibson named his dog in order to be offensive to black people! Much could be achieved with modern computer animation, including more convincing detonations at the dam walls. Yet, is it possible to create that air of authenticity, which did so much to underwrite the integrity of the 1950s film? I doubt it (although I would be happy to be proved wrong).

Nigger's grave at Scampton is fenced and well-tended, as is the grave of his illustrious master at a churchyard in The Netherlands. I have seen both. Gibson survived the Dams Raid but died the following year, alongside his Navigator, when their Mosquito went down. One can only ponder on the direction Gibson's life might have taken, had he lived. As for Douglas Bader, I remember him making the annual Battle of Britain "Wings Day" appeal, during a September visit to a cinema in the early 1980s. There he was, filling the cinema screen and reminding everyone of the sacrifice made by too many young men, who should have had their whole lives in front of them. It matters not that, in reality, Bader was a notoriously difficult man, blunt to the point of extreme rudeness. In his time as a prisoner, many thought that his extreme "Goon-baiting" was not necessarily in the best interests of fellow POWs in Colditz. All this counts as nothing against the man himself. If anyone wants a hero, look no further than Douglas Bader. He lived life to the full with what he had left (which proved to be quite enough). Bader was knighted in 1976 for services to the disabled. He died suddenly, in 1982.

Jack Hawkins made five war films yet, somehow, this number feels like an under-estimate. He epitomised the British officer of the best type: firm, fundamentally decent and with compassion flowing in his veins. His films, including *Angels One-Five* (1952), *The Cruel Sea* and *Malta Story* (1953), amount to an outstanding legacy. Hawkins was a heavy smoker; he was only 62 when he died of throat cancer.

---oOo---

- 13 -

Out To Play

Childhood was a more physical experience in the 1950s. Television may have captured our young minds, but the daily output was limited and there were no computer games or mobiles. My pockets were empty, beyond some chewing gum and a grubby handkerchief. Much of my free time was spent in Manor House Gardens, a few minutes walk away and known to all as "The Park". The Manor House was built in 1772 by Thomas Lucas. It was acquired in 1796 by Sir Francis Baring, who became wealthy dealing in American stocks during the War of Independence. Sir Francis continued to prosper and became Chairman of the East India Company. More recently, the family business, Baring Brothers, hit a rock thanks to the predatory activities of rogue trader Nick Leeson.

I was unaware that my playground was once Sir Francis' private garden. I knew the Manor House as the Library. The Baring family sold this impressive pile to Lewisham Borough Council in 1899. The house became a library and the grounds opened as a public park in 1902. The family also gave the site for Northbrook School to the Church. There is now an ugly new school (its third incarnation) on the site bordering what was our modest end-terraced home, 48 Hedgley Street.

The Baring family home: the Manor House became Lee Green's Library and its grounds became a public park, Manor House Gardens.

Manor House Gardens, with its ornamental lake, is bisected by the River Quaggy. This park was an idyllic place in the 1950s. Its wooden benches were occupied by old men in old suits, with flat caps and watch chains. With the benefit of hindsight, I now realise that they were probably not that old. Many had been maimed or gassed in the Great War and were too disabled to work. They passed the day sitting on the benches around the lake. They were silent for the most part, staring at the lake and its noisy armada of ducks. The lake was full of fish and some were extremely large. Dad contributed to its excessive population. When we children began to toddle, Dad filled in our garden's small fishpond. He picked his moment carefully and quietly tipped a bucketful of fish into the lake.

The view from the park benches: ducks on Manor House Gardens' lake.

During Summer weekends families gathered in the park, picnicking on the broad green. This open space was bordered by impressive trees, once the pride of the Baring household. Fathers in shirt-sleeves and grey flannels played cricket with their kids, as the evening sun cast a golden halo over what remained of the day.

When ten years old I was free to head for the park gates in Taunton Road whenever I wanted. The entrance was just around the corner, past the then new school (second incarnation) – built on what had been, until recently, a brick-strewn bombsite. I bounced my red plastic *Frido* football on the pavement as I walked. For some reason, I had absolutely no interest in football as a spectator sport. I never supported a team. To this day, I have never been to a football match. Yet I loved playing football on the large area of tarmac in the corner of the park bordering Northbrook School.

Teams were picked. Coats and sweaters were put down for goals. At one end of the "pitch" was a stout brick wall. This defined the garden boundaries of houses fronting onto Taunton Road – including the one once rented by my maternal grandparents. A high wire fence topped the wall but, occasionally, our ball soared over the top. It was impossible to climb over and retrieve it. If the ball went over, that was it: five shillings (25p) down the drain! I was no football star but played with enthusiasm. I was always one of the last to be picked for a team. Yet, even I was preferred to the unfortunate boy known as "Dopey", generally the last addition to any side.

Manor House Gardens made me aware of nature and the seasons. Sometimes I flopped down on my back, spread my arms in the grass and felt the Earth rotate. Summer clouds sailed by. Chemical farming had yet to kill off the wildlife. There were "sticky buds", catkins, sweet chestnuts, acorns, oak apples, butterflies, caterpillars and moths (especially Tiger Moths) and huge stag beetles – fearsome-looking creatures. I became aware of death. One Summer day I turned over a dead pigeon and was horrified to see that its underside was covered in maggots.

We waited for the conkers to ripen. We threw broken branches (or anything else) into the horse-chestnuts, to bring them down. In my view, getting conkers was more fun than playing conkers (which seemed slightly daft to me, even then).

Damaging park trees was a serious offence. A careful watch was essential, to avoid being caught. The park-keepers were based in a timber hut beside the small bridge over the Quaggy. They wore the rather odd brown serge uniforms provided by London County Council and were always on the watch for bad behaviour. "Nosy" (ie. "Nosy Parker") was lanky, young and not too interested in catching offenders. He preferred to drink tea in his hut or indulge in gentle gardening. "Crabapple", however, was a different kettle of fish. He was older, with a sour face (hence the moniker). My friend and I made a big mistake when we walked some yards ahead of him, turned and shouted "Crabapple". The offended park-keeper chased us to the park gate and, to our horror, carried on running! It took 10 breathless minutes to convince him that the chase was not worth the effort. From that day on he received more respect.

Long gone: the Park-keepers' hut once stood to the left of the picture, just beyond the tree on the banks of the River Quaggy.

"Crabapple": we shouted and pulled faces at a Park-keeper, who then chased us out of this gate and continued to run along Taunton Road. He was difficult to shake off.

I had a favourite tree to climb, but avoided going too high (given the need to beat a hasty retreat, should "Crabapple" come within range). I enjoyed rolling down the grassy hill beyond the lake. I had no idea that this "hill" covered the Baring family's ice house. Another diversion – the latest craze – involved holding my breath for as long as possible and then dropping quickly onto my haunches. This was meant to make you pass out. I can't remember how effective this was; I have thought of trying it now but I suspect that, at this stage in my life, it might work only too well!

During a Summer's evening in the park I saw some strange behaviour. A young man appeared to be lying on top of a girl. They looked very uncomfortable and it sounded as though the girl was complaining. I made the grave mistake of mentioning this to Mum, on returning home. She put on her coat, grabbed me and walked briskly to the park, to give "Nosy" an earful about allowing filthy behaviour in front of children. I had no idea what she was on about and stood well clear of the hut.

---ooo---

Games played in the park included "Bad Eggs" – sometimes involving a group of girls armed with a tennis ball. The ball was thrown high into the air by the player who was "it". This was the signal for everyone to scatter. When the ball was caught, "Bad Eggs!" was called and we froze. The ball was then thrown at those within range, who were "out" if struck.

In the school playground I spent most of my time as a Spitfire, arms fully extended. I gave my best impression of a Rolls Royce Merlin engine, punctuated by bursts of machine gun fire. There was also "Kiss Chase", a self-explanatory game. I became more enthusiastic about this after my tenth birthday. A few pupils indulged in mild sexual behaviour in the playground; I was aware of this but was far more interested in attacking the Luftwaffe with my Spitfire guns. Across the playground, girls with skirts tucked into their navy blue knickers were skipping, playing hopscotch or calling "Queeny, Queeny, who's got the ball?" Others chanted:

> "The farmer's in his den,
> The farmer's in his den,
> Heigh hi addy oh,
> The farmer's in his den".

Many commentaries on 1950s playground life mention "British Bulldog". This game would certainly fail a 21st-century health and safety assessment, given its scope for violence. One or two "Bulldogs" stood in the middle of a run of around 60 ft. On the shout "British Bulldogs – 1, 2, 3", everyone sought to complete the run without being caught by the Bulldogs. If you were tackled, kicked or punched and caught, you became a Bulldog.

The 17th Lewisham North Cub pack met in the school hall on Friday evenings. I loved Cubs. The fun began before the formal proceedings, as boys chased each other around the school cloakrooms. Cub games made the most of the school hall's highly polished pine block floor. "Rafts" was another 1950s game ignoring health and safety principles. We gathered at one end of the hall, then ran towards a large square marked out on the floor at the opposite end. After the first run the square – or "raft" – was made smaller. The pushing and shoving began at the next go and grew steadily worse. Those failing to board the raft "drowned" when the whistle blew and took no further part. This continued until two bruised Cubs struggled to get onto a raft just big enough for one.

"Kim's Game" was more sedate. This encouraged observation and retention of detail. A tray of objects, covered with a cloth, was uncovered for one minute. Each Cub memorised the items and wrote them down when the cover was back in place. The game took its name from Rudyard Kipling's 1901 novel – *Kim*, who played the game during his training as a spy. Today, many Special Forces include a form of Kim's Game in their training.

The kindly Mrs Pratt was our "Akela". I prospered in the Cubs, earning an armful of badges – including the "Leaping Wolf". I became a "Sixer". I then transferred to the Scouts and found it dreary by comparison. The best part of a Scout evening was its close. This was signalled by singing *Taps*, a tune attributed to the Union Army of the American Civil War. The final line of this haunting melody remains with me after more than 50 years: "All is well, safely rest. God is nigh".

During one particular Friday evening, however, God was busy elsewhere. There was an unusually violent thunderstorm, culminating in a cloudburst. The Cubs were held in the hall as torrential rain drummed at the windows. Lightning came every few seconds. Within 30 minutes the Quaggy flooded, turning Manor Lane into a fast-flowing river. Soaked parents began to arrive and Dad escorted me home. We were both impressed at the extent of the flooding.

It looks peaceful enough: the River Quaggy was prone to flooding in unusually heavy rainstorms.

As for the Scouts, I decided to leave after a miserable weekend spent camping in Knole Park, near Sevenoaks. I ate something that disagreed with me: a revolting dish of thin, hot custard sprinkled with chopped raw apple. This unattractive combination made me very sick indeed. Perhaps the milk was off?

---ooo---

It was easy to buy fireworks in the 1950s. Every newsagent sold *Paine's*, *Astra*, *Wessex* and others. *Golden Rain*, *Jack-in-a-Box*, *Mount Vesuvius* and countless other colourful pyrotechnics were sold loose from glass cabinets and in family boxes for eagerly-awaited Guy Fawkes Night.

I went with Dad to buy the fireworks. He bought a family box, together with half a dozen rockets and two packets of *Sparklers*. Would the evening be dry? We assumed it would as 5 November approached. Dad built a small bonfire on a flower bed, placed the nails ready for *Catherine Wheels* and found a milk bottle for launching the rockets.

Meanwhile, I collected money for a few more fireworks. I bought the ugliest available Guy mask, painted in lurid colours. Mum helped me stuff an old sack and stockings with newspaper, to form the head, body, arms and legs. I dragged my Guy to Lee Green's shopping parade and tried my luck with that age-old cry: "Penny for the Guy!" I did quite well and always managed to raise enough to buy some large *Roman Candles*.

Mum began preparing sausage sandwiches as night fell and the whizzes and bangs reverberated outside. We had mugs of warming tomato soup and went outside to enjoy the fun. Dad insisted that he alone set off the fireworks. The rockets were great, but the *Catherine Wheels* always got stuck. We twirled our *Sparklers* to make glowing circles in the cold night air. The fire crackled and released shoals of sparks. We ate our sausage sandwiches, tomato sauce leaking out over our fingers. Our breath was visible in the yellow glow of the fire.

I spent the next morning searching for "duds". I scoured the bombsite next door for spent rockets. The day after Guy Fawkes night always smelt of smoke and was bitterly cold. A thick, white layer of frost covered the ground and stung my fingers.

---ooo---

I have no idea what games are played in today's playgrounds. Yet my vegetable garden borders a junior school playground and the playtime noise penetrating the tall hedge sounds familiar and reassuring. My guess, however, is that girls no longer tuck their skirts into their knickers and boys do not run around pretending to be Spitfires. I am sure that British Bulldog is no more. God knows what the "New Puritans" would make of Kiss Chase.

As for the Cubs, "Bob-a-job Week" is long gone. Most people today don't know what a "Bob" is and, besides, 5p is a poor reward for mowing a lawn. "Bob-a-job Week", first known as "Good Turn Day", was introduced in 1914 by Scout Movement founder Lord Baden-Powell. Although a Cub Sixer, I had no idea that Bob-a-job Week was relatively new, having been launched during Easter 1949. It involved knocking on doors and offering to do domestic and other chores in return for a shilling. The beneficiaries received a window sticker displaying a large tick, to ensure they were not approached twice.

This scheme was axed in the 1990s, suffocated by health and safety and child protection laws. How can children be expected to knock on doors when any door could conceal a raging paedophile? "Scout Job Week", as it was then known, ended in the UK in 1992. It was resurrected 20 years on as "Scout Community Week", with a focus on volunteering and building "entrepreneurial skills and helpfulness". No money now changes hands!

Today's Chief Scout is TV danger man Bear Grylls – the man who free-falls into challenging environments and is prepared to eat anything. He is rather different from the 1950s role model, when the Scout movement was dominated by former military men who saw service during World War Two. Leadership styles have certainly changed over the decades.

---ooo---

During the 1980s Manor House Gardens looked a sorry sight. Park-keepers were nowhere to be seen. Flowerbeds were untended and trampled. Walls were covered in graffiti and many of the park's areas appeared to be wired off. One of South London's most charming small parks was in ruins. At that time, Manor House Gardens had a strange atmosphere – a blend of sadness and menace.

I looked at the lake, with its forlorn and rather stagnant appearance. I thought about our childish run-ins with the park-keepers of the 1950s. We may have misbehaved but we could at least be certain that, had we fallen into the lake when feeding the ducks, they would have jumped in to rescue us. Today, people have drowned in three feet of water or less, watched by firemen and policemen forbidden to intervene by health and safety rules.

More recently, efforts have been made to restore the park, which was rescued by Heritage Lottery funding. The old tearoom is now a modern cafe. The graffiti (most of it) has been removed. New, family-friendly areas have been established. Unfortunately, today's park users have not been similarly transformed. Whilst taking photographs for this book, I was accused of being a pervert by a gigantic, shaven-headed, heavily-tattooed father with an IQ of around 25 and a morbid fear of late middle-aged men armed with cameras. Ignoring the presence of his young family, he poured out a torrent of foul-mouthed abuse. Manor House Gardens may be "family-friendly", but are the families friendly? What, exactly, is everyone afraid of?

---ooo---

- 14 -

Freedom and The Family Car

....

"That's what we are getting!" I looked agog at the "sit up and beg" Ford on the opposite side of Taunton Road and replied to Dad: "That's very modern!" This might seem an odd response from a seven-year-old, but there were plenty of 1940s cars still around in early 1956 and a Ford *Popular* was modern at that time.

The Ford *Popular* lived up to its name. It was the UK's lowest-priced car when launched in 1953. This two-door saloon was produced until 1962 and over 150,000 were built. One example belonged to the Redding family. It was a very basic car, but GUN 481 was much loved. It took some time to get used to the idea that it was ours. It had a three-speed gearbox and its long gear lever was topped with a brown *Bakelite* knob. With a top speed of 60 mph, it accelerated from 0-50 mph in 24.1 seconds. Petrol consumption was 36.4 mpg. Cars of this type, although basic, were expensive to ordinary working men. A new Ford *Popular* cost £390 in 1954. Our example was second-hand but, as far as the kids were concerned, GUN 481 was big, black and beautiful.

Brew-up: Mum enjoys a cup of tea in the front seat of Ford Popular GUN 481.

---ooo---

During the 1950s Britain was the world's second largest car producer and the leading exporter. The British car industry made a remarkable recovery after World War

Two and a six-year break in production. The manufacturers building armoured vehicles and trucks quickly returned to the production of family saloons.

When the war ended, Britain's coffers were empty. It was a case of "export or die" and new vehicles went overseas to earn revenue. In 1947, only those vehicle manufacturers with 75 per cent export production or better received state-controlled steel supplies. Within a few years Britain was exporting more cars than any other nation and captured just over 50 per cent of the world market.

---ooo---

The car revolutionised our family life. Grey Sundays were enlivened by the chance to "go for a spin". Some of our trips to the country were made with the Prior family. Bert Prior was a bus driver. He and his wife, Win, also had a young family. Many of our Sunday drives were made in convoy with the Priors.

Polishing GUN 481, however, was a task I came to hate. I sweated beside its bulbous wheel arches, using wax from the round tin of *Simoniz*. Marketed as giving "a brilliant shine, with lasting protection", *Simoniz Original Car Wax* was said to be "quick and easy to use". I did not find it so. The polish was applied in swirls and dried into a powdery film highly resistant to elbow grease. The black paintwork could be buffed to a deep shine, but this required immense effort.

The engines of cars of this vintage were usually easy to work on – virtually everything was within easy reach. For some reason I learned nothing about car mechanics but I was aware that things could go wrong. I remember Dad complaining of a persistent slipping fan belt. Occasionally, the problems were more traumatic. I remember his horror when a Cornish garage told him that GUN 481's tappets had gone. Naturally, "tappets" meant nothing to me, but it was obvious that this trouble was serious and it took most of the family's hard-earned holiday money to fix. Some things were said to ward off gremlins – such as a shot of *Redex* at the garage – but it didn't work on that occasion.

---ooo---

During my walk to school I enjoyed spotting favourite cars, including a rakish 1940s black sports saloon. It looked rather like the sort of vehicle the Gestapo had used in France during the Occupation (which had ended barely a decade earlier). I loved the circular fairing on the boot, housing the spare wheel.

I liked black Police cars and those wonderful "tugs" at London railway stations –

three-wheeled tractors pulling trailers stacked with mailbags and freight. They bore an uncanny resemblance to giant locusts. Other favourites included steamrollers making their ponderous way from one road resurfacing job to another. They produced a peculiar "hollow" noise. The best vehicle to spot, however, was the "drain lorry", its proboscis – a long, counterbalanced arm – stowed across its tank during transit.

The greatest vehicle of all, however, was my Dad's lorry. He was a track welder and, occasionally, he and his railway "mate" would drive their lorry from job to job. As a small child I accompanied them from time to time, spending most of the night shift asleep in the cab. I loved sitting between the men as they drove this ancient long-nosed petrol lorry. My perch was a cushion on top of the battery box. I can still remember that distinctive whine as the lorry pulled away.

---ooo---

Britain, once the world's largest car exporter, now ranks twelfth in the league table. Many British car marques are foreign-owned. The rights to many dormant brands, such as *Riley* and *Triumph*, are now owned by foreign companies. Yet the late 1950s was a time of great promise in the world of British car manufacturing. The highlight was the 1959 launch of Alec Issigonis' *Mini*, for BMC. The breath-taking *E-type* Jaguar was just two years away.

Today, the names of inactive marques have the ring of poetry. They include *Alvis, Austin, Hillman, Morris, Riley, Rover, Singer, Standard, Sunbeam* and *Wolseley*.

The "sit up and beg" soon disappeared. New trends were underlined by the *Mini* and the 105E Ford *Anglia*, with its strange, inward sloping rear window. I remember staring at a 105E in a car showroom window. It was SO DIFFERENT that it could only be described as startling. The new Ford *Anglia* (the fourth incarnation of the name) stayed in production for eight years; nearly one million were built.

In 1962, however, my Dad went for the new Ford *Popular*, the 100E. This was still a three-speed car but the top speed had risen to a nippy 69.9 mph. Acceleration to 50 mph was 19.6 seconds. The gear stick knob was now of white plastic, rather than *Bakelite*. Fuel consumption was 33.2 mpg. In 1960 a new 100E cost £494, equivalent to around half the average annual UK wage. Manufacturers of popular family cars retained this broad price relationship with average earnings for many years.

---ooo---

- 15 -

Out and About...

It was possible to have a good evening out in Lee Green during the 1950s without fear of being mugged, raped or seeing your children kidnapped by paedophile gangs. We made regular trips to Lewisham and Sunday outings to Greenwich Park, both only a mile or so from home. Greenwich Park's attractions included the deer, the tearooms by the bandstand, the imposing statue of General Wolfe and the even more impressive view down to the river from the hilltop Royal Observatory.

My parents enjoyed the occasional Friday or Saturday night out at "Jimmy's". Jimmy, an ex-boxer, was the landlord of *The Duke of Edinburgh*, a popular Lee Green pub beside the River Quaggy. I remember watching Dad get ready, standing in his white vest and shaving at the sink upstairs. The evening sun streamed into the small room and its light fell across his well-muscled torso. He patted his face dry and put on his favourite shirt, its cream, silky material covered in a small diamond pattern.

On Summer weekend evenings the kids were outside Jimmy's, enjoying lemonade and *Smith's Crisps*. The salt in that twist of blue waxed paper was always damp, preventing its even distribution in my bag of crisps. Sometimes I asked for cream soda; I loved its soft, sweet taste. A warm noise floated out from the pub door, as the grown-ups enjoyed a sing-song around the upright piano: *You made*

"Jimmy's": the Duke of Edinburgh was a popular venue for sing-songs around the piano. The area occupied by the two vans was the kids' area in the 1950s. We would drink lemonade, polish off our crisps and throw stones into the River Quaggy below.

me love you, Bye-bye, blackbird, Show me the way to go home. We were never bored, being content to sip our fizzy drinks and throw stones into the Quaggy's shallows.

---ooo---

Everything changed when the family car came along. Suddenly, country pubs were within easy reach. Sixty years ago the countryside was not far away from Lee Green and there was no sign of "suburban creep". Traffic was light and parking was straightforward. There were no parking meters or ticket machines. We parked anywhere, without difficulty – no-one gave parking a second thought.

Picnic: Dad, Mum and Janet sit out beside GUN 481.

Our Sunday outings included morning fishing trips to Keston Ponds, near Bromley. Mum and Nan stayed at home to prepare lunch (Sunday dinner). Keston was entirely rural in the 1950s and the Ponds had an unusual, brooding atmosphere. Dense woods – including many large, ancient trees – surrounded the spring-fed fishponds and Caesar's Well, the source of the River Ravensbourne.

Keston's large fishponds were constructed in the early 19th-century. By the 1950s this popular fishing venue was always crowded on Sunday mornings. The surface of the water was covered in brightly coloured floats. The floor of the ponds must have been carpeted in a dense layer of drowned maggots and worms. I had little in the way of fishing tackle: a small, almost useless fibreglass rod and a sturdier, short sea rod that looked out of place at Keston. It was difficult to cast out and avoid water lilies and other anglers' lines. Few people caught fish at Keston. I can remember catching just the one. A small jack pike's greed overcame the natural reluctance of all Keston fish to oblige, in the face of their daily barrage of floats, weights, hooks and baits. Hooking something was a real shock! Kids fishing nearby came over to

Prize catch: The author's brother, Colin, proudly holds up the Pike from Keston Ponds.

help or simply to gawp. I had nothing to take the hook out, perhaps reflecting my pessimistic view of fishing at Keston. We took this hapless pike home. It was put in the tin bath in the back garden, much to Mum's annoyance. The fish soon expired.

My young sister, Janet, caused a sensation at Keston. There was an area of very shallow water near our car. Dad was distracted and failed to notice as Janet approached the water, which was covered in an unbroken carpet of bright green duckweed. She assumed this was grass, kept walking and then screamed. Dad moved fast. Wading in, he scooped her up and lifted her onto dry land. This took just seconds but Janet was already plastered with mud and duckweed. Dad took her to the back of the car, stripped off her wet clothes and wrapped her in a blanket. We headed for home. All this took some explaining – Mum was not impressed.

---ooo---

Many Sunday outings involved the delightful River Darent. The source of this small, spring-fed river is just south of Westerham. The Darent flows for 21 miles, past Otford, Shoreham, Lullingstone roman villa, Eynsford, Farningham, Horton Kirby, South Darenth, Sutton-at-Hone, Darenth and on to Dartford.

Eynsford, a charming village, has an ancient packhorse bridge over the Darent. During 1940 the ford alongside the bridge was blocked by a haycart and barrels, to deter German tanks. Sixteen years on, in 1956, Eynsford was a peaceful, watery playground for small children. The clear, shallow stream ran swiftly over the ford's gravel bed. Kids splashed around, using fishing nets to chase glittering shoals of Minnows and Gudgeon. Mums and Dads sat on canvas picnic chairs or sprawled on blankets along the grassy bank, the men enjoying pints from the pub near the bridge. The kids' excited laughter filled the air. This river was full of small fish, including young trout. Taking small trout home was a big mistake. They were always dead the next morning, having jumped out of the bowl overnight.

Dad sometimes headed out of Eynsford village, following the narrow lane leading to Lullingstone roman villa. Here, the river teemed with small trout. We threw in bread and followed it in the swift current, as it was attacked by hordes of fish. They drifted obligingly into the waiting net, to be scooped up for inspection and eventual return to the sparkling stream.

A roman villa held little interest for small boys. The river provided the real fun. A few years later Dad took fishing rods on trips to Eynsford. A single maggot, suspended under a small bob float, attracted the larger fish in the silver shoals. Occasionally, we put the rods away and set out on a walk, to pick wild flowers in the Eynsford lanes. Sometimes we had company, being joined by the Priors: Uncle Bert, Aunty Win and their three kids. We would drive to nearby Knatts Valley, a favourite spot for picnics and blackberrying. We took a packed lunch and never paid for a meal out! We had sandwiches, cake and orange drinks for the children.

Horton Kirby, also on the Darent, was another frequent destination. Horton Kirby's fishing lakes were in a raw state at that time, due to recent gravel working. The banks consisted of patchy grass and stone. With no shelter around, it was easy to get soaked in a sudden shower. Once again, I don't remember catching much.

---ooo---

My favourite outing was to the Battle of Britain airfield of Biggin Hill, near Bromley, on the Westerham road. Less than 20 years before, in that dangerous Summer of 1940, Biggin Hill played a central role in defeating the Luftwaffe raids. This base was a "Sector Station" for RAF Fighter Command's No. 11 Group. It is just 14 miles from the centre of the capital its pilots so valiantly defended. The station crest, a fighting sword, carried the motto: *The strongest link*.

Biggin Hill's success continued after the great air battles of 1940. During World War Two its fighters claimed 1,400 enemy aircraft. This success came at a heavy price; 453 Biggin Hill aircrew lost their lives fighting for freedom. The airfield was bombed repeatedly – it was attacked 25 times in the period 18 August, 1940, to 19/20 April, 1941. The hilltop airfield enjoyed an iconic status. The scars of bombing were still visible in the surrounding woods during the 1950s. The *White Hart*, a pub at nearby Brasted, proudly displayed a blackout screen with the chalked signatures of fighter aces such as Bob Tuck, "Sailor" Malan, Tony Bartley, Brian Kingcome, Al Deere and many others who flew from "Biggin on the Bump". This was the most famous fighter station in the world; how could a small boy not be interested in such a place?

After the war Biggin Hill continued as a fighter base. Its squadrons graduated from *Spitfires* to *Meteor* jets and, later, *Hawker Hunters*. With the new threat from Russian long-range bombers, however, Britain's air defences shifted north. Biggin Hill lost its operational status in 1958. The aircraft departed and the base became the RAF's Aircrew Selection Centre. There was still plenty of flying, but only occasional military traffic. The airfield developed as a busy centre for light aviation when Croydon (London's original airport) closed in 1959. Yet there were plenty of military jets around at least once a year. They gathered every September for Biggin Hill's spectacular "Battle of Britain Day" air display. During the 1950s huge crowds attended the airshow, held as close as possible to 15 September (the climax of the 1940 air battles over Kent and London).

These displays were spectacular. Whole squadrons of front-line RAF aircraft participated! I remember watching a squadron of delta-winged *Gloster Javelin* fighters taxi out for their display. Then came the chest-squeezing roar of four powerful *Bristol Olympus* engines as a much larger delta – the *Avro Vulcan* V-Bomber – passed low overhead and banked into a steep climb. The crowd felt, rather than heard, its fierce wave of noise. Later, a development of these engines powered *Concorde*. In 1958 I would have laughed at the idea that, many years on, I would fly at Mach 2 in a supersonic airliner.

A squadron of *English Electric Lightning* fighters made the biggest impression. I watched, open-mouthed, as a full squadron of these supersonic jets took off for their display. This opened with a fantastic afterburner climb. One by one, the *Lightnings* rolled along the runway, rotated and entered a near vertical climb, sitting on a long red tongue of afterburner flame. The noise was physical – like a punch to the body. Everyone present regarded the RAF as great value for money. I certainly did!

The precision display by 111 Squadron's all-black *Hunters* was another highlight. The *Black Arrows* were the predecessors of today's *Red Arrows*. "Treble One" still holds a record: in 1958 22 *Hunters* looped at the Farnborough Air Show. I missed this, but I saw the *Black Arrows* at Biggin Hill. A colour photograph of 16 black *Hunters*, in perfect diamond formation, had pride of place on my bedroom mantelpiece. I had no doubts about my future. All I could think about was reaching Biggin Hill's Aircrew Selection Centre. Sadly, I was rather young for such challenges. I had to be content with a photograph taken standing in front of a *Spitfire* and *Hurricane* – Biggin Hill's proud "Gate Guardians".

Thumbs up: the Redding and Prior families (Bert Prior took the photo), in front of one of Biggin Hill's "Gate Guardians".

These fighters of yesteryear had pride of place in front of St George's Chapel of Remembrance, built in 1951 to replace the Biggin Hill Station Church (which had been destroyed by fire five years earlier). It was fitting that Air Chief Marshal Lord Dowding, victor of the Battle of Britain, laid the new chapel's foundation stone. The chapel is a memorial to those killed during the Battle of Britain and those who died later, flying from Biggin Hill. Inscribed oak panels to each side of the altar list the station's dead during World War Two, together with the badges of 52 RAF squadrons. There are also remarkable stained glass windows by Hugh Easton, installed in 1953 and representing the winged spirits of the pilots. An illuminated Roll of Honour lists those pilots killed whilst serving at Biggin Hill.

---ooo---

Leaves Green is on the edge of Biggin Hill airfield, alongside the Westerham Road. It was one of our favourite Summer picnic spots. The bushes at the back of this grassy expanse provided excellent blackberrying during the late Summer. Having picked bags of juicy black fruit, our hands stained purple and sore from the thorns, we walked down the farm track leading into the valley. At a point just below the top of the slope, we spread our blankets and unpacked the food. The kids shot off to explore chalky craters left by a stick of German bombs in 1940 (or so we imagined).

There was always a deep, rich odour of animal dung as we walked down the Leaves Green track and passed the farmyard. Mum would mutter: "Ah! That fresh country air!" Lazy in the sun, we laid in the valley's long grass, full of wild flowers and exotic insects. In the background was the constant drone of light aircraft, in circuit around the airfield. Leaves Green, at that time, was one of the jewels of Kent.

---ooo---

School journeys cost money. Consequently, I made only the one excursion. I spent a week at Sayer's Croft Field Centre, near Ewhurst, Surrey. I joined the large party from Lee Manor Junior School boarding two coaches. There was a crescendo of noise from over-excited 10-year-olds as we pulled away. This was my first separation from home and parents.

Sayer's Croft was built as a haven for child evacuees from Catford. I had a wonderful week. The weather was warm and every day was crammed with activities. We climbed Leith Hill, which felt like Everest to my young legs. We made crude pots from raw yellow clay dug from a nearby stream bank. We played organised games or simply chased each other across a wide grass field, into the dense woods fringing the site. The bushes at the edge of the wood attracted large populations of butterflies, including Tortoiseshells, Peacocks, Red Admirals and Purple Emperors.

At the end of the day, happy and exhausted, we settled into our large, timber-built dormitories. During the week I went down with a stomach upset. I was put to bed in the Sick Bay, sorry to miss out on that day's events but comfortable enough. Unfortunately, by this time Mum could no longer tolerate my absence and cajoled Dad into driving down to visit me. This was against all the rules – no visits from parents were permitted at Sayer's Croft. I now had to cope with diarrhoea *and* the embarrassment of an unauthorised parental visit. I got over both within a few hours and celebrated by consuming my holiday hoard of three *Bandit* chocolate wafers.

---ooo---

Now in my sixties, I make occasional visits to Lee Green. Things that once looked so big to a child's eyes now seem remarkably small. Lee Green today has a different atmosphere – more like an inner London Borough than a suburban "London village". Lee Green's pubs are now merely venues for a drink and a sandwich after family funerals. The personalities who played such an important part in my 1950s life are long gone. Jimmy's, *The Duke of Edinburgh*, is still open, but with no upright piano... and no Jimmy.

I have several wind-up gramophones and a large collection of 1930s and 1940s Dance Band records. These songs of my infancy have wonderful, evocative melodies: *Love is the sweetest thing, Put your arms around me, honey, Take good care of yourself – you belong to me.* Each 78 rpm record costs around £1 – a cheap ticket for a trip on a time machine!

Those Summer Sunday destinations have seen much change and not always for the worse. Horton Kirby's fishing lakes were devoid of trees and shrubs in the 1950s. The shingle banks and thin grass made the scene look rather raw. Today, however, these lakes are fringed by mature trees, creating a softer and more attractive vista. Eynsford is as pretty as ever. One Summer's day in 2009 I had the notion that a visit to Eynsford would bring me closer to Dad, who had died four years earlier. I was disappointed. I found no sign of Dad and was shocked at the state of the river. It still ran swiftly over the ford's gravel bed, but there were no shoals of tiddlers. Elsewhere, the river was low and slow-flowing over a silty bottom. The Darent had been ruined by over-abstraction. A crisis point was reached in 1989, when it was named as the river with the lowest flow in the country. The river's wildlife had been sacrificed – so much for the "Department of the Environment"! It took many years to repair the damage. A plan was devised to restore the river and the Environment Agency closed down many boreholes. A sculpture was unveiled in 2004 to celebrate the Darent's rejuvenation. Yet, those with memories of the 1950s Darent know it is not the same river.

As for Keston Ponds, I re-visited the place in the early 1980s. Then one of my college friends parked up under those large trees and gassed himself. Huge carp might still cruise the thick weed and lily beds at Keston, but they are welcome to it! I will not return to that haunted place.

---ooo---

The RAF are long gone from Biggin Hill but the Memorial Chapel and the *Spitfire* and *Hurricane* remain. Biggin Hill Airport is now a busy centre for general and business aviation. I have been diverted once or twice to Biggin Hill, when fog closed London City Airport. It felt odd to land at a former frontline fighter station, wearing a business suit and surrounded by irate passengers busy on their mobile phones, arranging for cars to pick them up. The Council purchased Biggin Hill Airport in 1974. The RAF presence ended in 1992, when the Aircrew Selection Centre moved to Cranwell. The Memorial Chapel is open seven days a week, but the *Spitfire* and *Hurricane* are now glass fibre replicas. I remember the real Gate Guardians. *Spitfire* SL674 arrived at Biggin Hill on 11 September, 1954. It was built in 1945 and served with two Royal Auxiliary Air Force squadrons. Faithful to the last, it stood by the Chapel until early 1989, when its glass fibre replacement arrived. Biggin Hill's *Spitfire* and *Hurricane* were too precious to be left outside. *Spitfire* SL674 was in poor condition, but its wings were good and they were later fitted to another *Spitfire* Gate Guardian (MK356, from RAF Locking). The latter then flew with the *Battle of Britain Memorial Flight*.

An additional show – Biggin Hill International Air Fair – was launched in the early 1960s, the flying programme featuring both military and civil aircraft. In that first year my devoted Dad took me to the May display and the traditional September event. In return, I prayed hard for fine weather. A wet day meant a more limited, low-level display. Even this was exciting to watch. When the low-flying fighters tight-turned at speed, a halo of water vapour bulged around their cockpits.

Battle of Britain Day at Biggin Hill is now a distant memory and the International Air Fair is also history. In July 2010 Biggin Hill Airport Ltd cancelled its contract with Air Displays International (just a few weeks after a record attendance at what was to be the last Air Fair). Biggin Hill's grand air pageants have been replaced with a more modest "Open House Air Day".

Biggin Hill retains its special atmosphere. If an airfield can be said to have such a thing, Biggin Hill has *presence*. It saw glory and tragedy in 1940. In one particularly severe raid, 39 people were killed on the ground. There then followed that sad, steady attrition of wartime pilots. Here today, gone tomorrow! When the war finished, tragedy continued to stalk Biggin Hill. On 18 June, 1953, three *Meteor* jets crashed, killing the pilots. An aircraft of 41 Squadron went out of control and two *Meteors* of 600 Squadron collided as they orbited the crash site. On 15 May, 1977, during the Air Fair, a *Bell* helicopter collided with a *Tiger Moth*. The biplane landed safely but all five on board the helicopter died. I witnessed one of Biggin Hill's many accidents. It happened during the Battle of Britain display on 21 September, 1980. A *Douglas A-26 Invader* was attempting a climbing roll when its nose dropped. It continued rolling as it fell vertically into the steep valley. I heard no sound but saw the ugly, brownish plume of smoke rise from the crash site, hidden from view in the valley below. Everyone around me stood still and stared. Nothing was said. Other fatal crashes at Biggin Hill in recent years include the losses of a *de Havilland Vampire* and a *Bell P-63 Kingcobra*, on successive days, at an air display in early June 2001. Another accident, on 30 March, 2008, killed five in a *Cessna Citation*.

Today, Biggin Hill is a familiar name to countless air passengers, being one of London Heathrow's four principal "stack" areas. Aircraft flying in from the south-east often circle Biggin Hill, waiting for clearance to join the Heathrow approach.

As for *Treble One Squadron*, it went on to operate a succession of powerful fighter types: *Lightnings*, *Phantoms* and *Tornado F3s*. Today, the people of Biggin Hill are proud of their heritage. The village sign consists of three aircraft – a *Hurricane* and two *Spitfires* – rising up into the rays of the sun.

---ooo---

Over 50 years after my brief Summer stay, Sayer's Croft continues as a field centre, specialising in outdoor and environmental education. Its current aims harmonise with those of the 1950s: "...to encourage understanding, appreciation, enjoyment and care of the natural environment, especially amongst children and young people and those who are disadvantaged". There is plenty of fun to be had at the modern Sayer's Croft. Facilities include a climbing wall, archery, abseiling, canoeing and orienteering, together with a 27-acre nature reserve.

Those timber huts, built in 1939—40, still provide comfortable accommodation for children who stay for a few days or a week. Sadly, however, the bushes fringing the woods no longer harbour Purple Emperor butterflies.

---ooo---

− 16 −

The Joys Of Cornwall

I opened the gate, stumbling as the dog pulled me through. Dad remarked: "Only two weeks to go. We'll soon be on holiday!" No-one we knew took their holidays abroad in the 1950s. For most, the only hope of travelling overseas was to join the forces and pray for a war. Package holidays and cheap flights were still many years away. Our destination in 1955 was Cornwall – a place apart. This was recognised over 1,000 years earlier, when Athelstan set the boundary between England and Cornwall on the Tamar.

Tourism rescued the Cornish economy after World War Two. The region had long been one of the poorest in Britain. Before the railways came, the Cornish relied on tin and copper mining, farming and fishing. The mines closed, the Pilchards disappeared but tourists were dependable; they flocked to Cornwall every Summer.

Our family's links to Cornwall originated in war, when my father, a Londoner, ended up in the *Duke of Cornwall's Light Infantry*. Jack became close friends with Cornishman Maurice Stribley. The ties between the Redding and Stribley families were to endure beyond their lifetimes.

Seventy years ago the two dark and handsome young conscripts, Jack and Maurice, were nicknamed "Blackout" and "Blackness". The wives got to know each other and Em and Joan kept in touch when their men went overseas. Maurice's *DCLI* Battalion sailed for the Middle East, whilst my father's Battalion went to the Far East. Maurice and Jack both endured great hardships, but in different ways. Maurice was captured and spent the rest of the war as a prisoner of the Germans. Jack went to India and became one of Wingate's Chindits, landing behind Japanese lines in a glider and surviving that bitter campaign in the Burmese jungle.

---ooo---

Both men returned and renewed their friendship. The families began to holiday together. We had no car but Dad worked for Southern Railway. "Privilege Tickets" were our passport to Cornwall and we travelled in style, with reserved seats on *The*

"Blackout" and "Blackness": Maurice Stribley (left) and Dad relax on leave from the Duke of Cornwall's Light Infantry.

Cornish Riviera Express. This crack train was named in a competition organised in 1904 by *Railway Magazine.* The Editor offered a prize of three guineas (£3.15). The 1,286 entries included *The Cornish Riviera Limited* and *The Riviera Express.* These ideas were combined, but railwaymen always knew *The Cornish Riviera Express* as *The Limited.*

We took the suburban train to London and made our annual cab ride to Paddington, entering that pungent world of noise, bustle and steam. There was that peculiar, hollow clanking noise made by slow-moving express locomotives manoeuvring into position. *The Limited's* carriages were resplendent in *Great Western* cream and chocolate. Negotiating the narrow corridor we entered our compartment and absorbed the odour of old cigarette smoke, dust and an unmistakable, pleasant smell of steam railway. The generously sprung bench seating was finished in dull green moquette. We pulled down the upholstered arms and switched on the small wall lights, as the station was dark. Our adventure began.

---ooo---

The big *King Class* locomotive's power was a physical presence, the rhythm of the ride interrupted by a swishing roar as we hurtled through small stations. I watched through the window. Telephone wires nodded up and down from post to post, the hypnotic effect broken by scudding clouds of smoke and steam. My parents were dozing as I crept out into the corridor. I opened the window at the far end of the carriage, leant out and caught sight of the *King* as it snorted into a bend. Truly, my ticket was a "privilege!"

Back in the compartment I rubbed my eyes, sore from smuts blown back in the slipstream. Mum stirred and assembled our packed lunch. I opened the grease-proof paper and sampled a cheese and tomato sandwich. It tasted somewhat fermented, having been made hours earlier, on a warm day. Things looked up with triangles of processed cheese – everyone wanted the tomato-flavoured triangle. There was orange squash and a gigantic *Wagon Wheel* which looked great but tasted rather stale. I munched away as we sped on towards that promised land of surf and sand. I stared at the posters by the wall lights – paintings of holidaymakers on Cornish beaches.

I was fortunate enough to travel on *The Cornish Riviera Express* in its final glory years, before steam surrendered to diesel. The 175th anniversary of the *GWR* (the *Great Western Railway* or, as some would have it, *God's Wonderful Railway*) was celebrated in 2010. On Saturday 26 June the 80-year-old *King Edward I* took *The Cornish Riviera Express* out of Paddington, bound for Penzance. Somehow, this commemorative event passed me by; had I known, I would have been on board.

Fifty-five years earlier, we gathered up our luggage as the express pulled into Par. We stood on the platform and waited for the Newquay branch line train. We were about to travel back in time, finding seats in ancient carriages drawn by a small locomotive. Newquay's passenger service had opened in 1876 and things had changed little over the years. The branch line linking Par to Newquay, just over 20 miles away, offered a charming railway experience. The small train entered the steep, heavily-wooded Luxulyan Valley and ran along the fast-flowing River Par, milk-white with suspension from the nearby China Clay works. I opened the window, struggling with the stiff leather belt, and stared at the white torrent.

Uncle Maurice was waiting at St Columb Road – a quaint halt amounting to little more than a sign and a couple of gas lamps. Maurice's soft Cornish burr underlined the warmth of his welcome. The bottle green *Morris Eight* stood ready. We squeezed in for the three-mile drive along the high-banked lanes leading to Summercourt.

---ooo---

Summercourt, five miles south-east of Newquay, is a village clustering around an ancient crossroads formed by the A30 and the Newquay to St Austell road. Summercourt's Charter Fair, the oldest in Cornwall, has its roots in the 11th-century Bodmin Long Fayre (which moved to Summercourt in the early 14th-century). This quiet, sleepy village has a pub, a shop, a Methodist Church and a village school founded in 1828.

I have dim early memories of Laurel Cottage, the Stribley home. Cob-built, with long, low rooms, it lacked all conventional comforts. There were no services; water was drawn from the garden well. There was no electricity or gas and oil lamps filled the rooms with a warm yellow glow. The toilet was in a small garden shed. The earth closet's harvest improved Maurice's large potato crop – surplus spuds were sold to supplement the family's income. From the front garden, looking towards St Austell, Cornwall's "pyramids" gleamed in the distance – sharp white peaks of waste from the China Clay workings.

Laurel Cottage had a distinct, pleasant aroma – a mix of polish, honey and... Cornwall. The local authority, however, was unimpressed. In the mid-1950s the Council declared it unfit and Maurice, Joan and their family of five moved to Beaconside. This new development, on the Newquay side of Summercourt's crossroads, consisted of plain yet comfortable new houses with mains water and electricity. They were built along three sides of a rectangle, set back from the Newquay road. The central, grassed area became a playground for kids.

Somehow, that wonderful, homely scent of Laurel Cottage migrated into the new Stribley home. Beaconside became our Cornish holiday base and a total of eight children made it a lively place. Tony and Maureen Stribley were the eldest. There were natural pairings between the other children. My counterpart was Christopher. My brother, Colin, was matched in age (and temperament) by David. My sister, Janet, was complemented by Annette.

Our space was the front bedroom, its windows overlooking the grassy playground below. During the evenings the families often went for a drink at the *London Inn*. Maurice and Jack reminisced over the *Duke of Cornwall's* and the war. Dad imitated the deep, booming voice of Sergeant-Major "Tipper" Hicks, giving his infamous command: "Put him in the dungeon!" Dad suffered Tipper's wrath when an inspection revealed beer in his water bottle. The two men teased each other over their pints. Maurice offered to show the children his bullet wounds. Dad laughed, muttering that he would have suffered more in Burma and adding: "You gave up after a couple of days!" Maurice rolled up a shirt sleeve and protested: "They left me for dead!" With Maurice's upper arm exposed, my Dad then shouted: "There you are! That's no bullet wound. That's your smallpox vaccination!" This harmless ritual was repeated every Summer.

Life at Beaconside revolved around the large kitchen. The front parlour – a formal room – was little used. There were four bedrooms and a generous garden. Maurice's large potato beds were now manured by conventional means. Chickens obliged with breakfast eggs. The high, stone-built wall at the bottom of the garden was smothered in honeysuckle and wild flowers, supported by armies of bees and butterflies. We peeped over the wall and spied on the pigs in the adjoining field.

---ooo---

St Enoder's Church, a short walk from Summercourt crossroads, is set back along a narrow lane off the London Road. This Grade l church casts a spell on the visitor. Squat walls emerge naturally from the ground, the stones enriched with patches of yellow, cream and rust coloured lichen. Generations of Stribleys have been baptised, married and buried here. This 14th-century church has 15th-century additions. The tower collapsed in 1684 but was rebuilt in 1711. The building still had an earth floor in the 1820s. Treasures within include the Flamank memorial – Thomas Flamank was a leader of the 1497 Cornish rebellion. The south aisle has a fine Norman font, where my brother, Colin, was christened during the Summer of 1951. Joan Stribley was his Godmother.

Behind the church, the lanes have stone banks festooned with foxgloves and honeysuckle, their blossoms worked by clouds of bees. The air is rich with the scent of dairy herd and the lanes are splashed with dark pools of thick, liquid dung. We threw stones into the brook and startled trout flashed past. There were mushrooms to pick in the heavily manured fields.

---ooo---

The kids prayed for sunny weather and lived for the next visit to Newquay's beaches, the golden sand and Atlantic rollers being just five miles away. Newquay's beaches, claimed as the finest in Europe, have evocative names: Fistral, Towan, Tolcarne and Lusty Glaze, with Crantock and Watergate Bay beyond. Newquay in the 1950s was full of family holidaymakers. Shops sold brightly painted "tin" buckets and spades, fishing nets and lilos. Surfboards were available for hire but were nothing like those of today. The 1950s surfboard was of thin ply with an upturned end. The idea was to "ride the waves", lying prone on the board. No-one thought of trying to stand up! Newquay was described as Britain's best "surf-riding" resort.

Cafes offered trays of tea for the beach. The tea washed down plump pasties. The kids licked canary yellow Cornish ice cream cones, biting off the bottom to use as a scoop. We staked out a pitch on the sand. Deckchairs and windbreaks were organised. The kids kicked up a fuss, impatient to get into the sea. Cornwall has been said to be "washed by a warm sea", but this is less than truthful. The sea *always* took my breath away! The trick was to wade in and jump as the next big wave approached. Occasionally, waves combined and broke unexpectedly into a thick mass of advancing white foam, dragging the unwary off their feet and along the sandy bottom. Each salty spill added to the thrills as the next roller began to curl.

Some beaches are more dangerous than others. I must have been about nine when, returning from the water's edge, I saw an agitated crowd ahead. I drew closer, peered through the ring of adults and saw someone desperately trying to revive a drowned man. He was a victim of Fistral's huge waves and fierce undercurrent.

It was warm and snug behind our windbreak. Shivering as I dried off inside a large towel wrap, there was just time to grab a drink and some crisps before setting off to build a dam across a rivulet snaking through the sands. We searched for seashells and explored rock pools, chasing shrimp, crabs and small fish with our nets. Gulls screamed overhead. Suddenly, a huge *Avro Shackleton* aircraft appeared, low above the waves. The maritime reconnaissance *Shackletons* – descendants of the wartime *Lancasters* – were based at nearby RAF St Mawgan.

Very impressive: an Avro Shackleton maritime reconnaissance bomber on the perimeter track at RAF St Mawgan.

Every Cornish beach has its unique characteristics. Porth, just beyond Newquay, is reached by a narrow road bridge across a stream. Our deckchairs and windbreaks were pitched against the concrete apron, to one side of that small stream crossing the sand. Maurice and Jack rolled up their sleeves and trousers; shoes and socks were discarded. Joan and Em were already wearing one-piece swimsuits equipped with "modesty aprons".

Porth Beach held many attractions. We waded into the stream, moved under the road bridge and caught silver sand eels in our nets. The tide receded, revealing a vast expanse of yellow sand. We could now reach the rocks at the cliff bottom, to examine large, deep rock pools. There were razor shells and gull feathers to collect.

Enjoying the sun: relaxing on Porth Beach, near Newquay – Joan and Maurice Stribley and Dad, with some of the kids (David, Janet and Annette). Note the tray of tea.

We returned to camp, where the windbreaks flapped briskly in the breeze. As the wind freshened, foam was stripped from the shallows and rolled along the sand like tumbleweed. There was a continuous, distant booming as the breakers surged in.

Tony Stribley was adventurous. He explored Porth's huge caves and deep pools, then climbed for gulls' eggs. The other kids stayed in the water, ignoring the cold and their white, wrinkled hands.

In later years, as we grew older, parental discipline was relaxed. On occasion we abused our new freedoms. Colin and I walked along a sandy beach one Summer afternoon, then took the lane up the hill and attempted a short cut. This was a poor decision. We were just over halfway across the field when we saw the bull, standing in one corner. Deeply resenting this intrusion, the animal responded with a full charge and we reached the safety of the far gate only just in time.

On one occasion, a year or two later, we missed the last bus from Newquay to Summercourt and set out to walk as the sun went down. Colin became increasingly nervous as it grew darker. As we passed a farm gate, my brother shrieked when an unseen cow let out a sudden, deep bellow. He took off at full speed and only stopped when out of oxygen. We reached Beaconside safe and sound, where stern reprimands were tempered with obvious relief.

---ooo---

Our outings usually included a trip to Padstow, then a much quieter place. The harbour's restaurants and cafes offered pasties, fish and chips, crab sandwiches and not much else (Rick Stein's *Seafood Restaurant* was still two decades away). On one occasion Joan and Em visited Padstow's quayside toilets. The lifeboat maroon suddenly soared into the sky and exploded directly overhead, followed by the shriek of the siren. Panic-stricken, the ladies fled the building in a state of undress.

Dad occasionally and reluctantly agreed to a short fishing trip. He hated boats and almost always felt seasick. He preferred driving along the Cornish lanes, although he was nervous of the narrowest byways. Maurice led the way in his new *Mayflower*, rounding blind bends and splashing through shallow fords which took the unsuspecting Londoners by surprise.

We visited Perranporth, with its four miles of beach and sand dunes. I caused a major scare when I became lost in the dunes whilst chasing butterflies. Harlyn Bay, just west of Padstow, had a Neolithic cemetery. As small boys we stared at the ghastly skeletons in their glass-topped graves, fascinated but filled with distaste. We preferred Harlyn's fine beach, or a trip across Bodmin Moor to the *Jamaica Inn* – the setting for Daphne du Maurier's novel – to enjoy lemonade and crisps.

---ooo---

In 1956, having acquired a car, we drove to Cornwall for the first time. The bulging roof rack was covered in a tarpaulin and tightly lashed down. Mum ticked off her list of towns as we advanced as quickly as our three-speed Ford *Popular*, GUN 481, would allow. The spectre of car sickness hovered over the back seat and regular comfort breaks were essential. Our first stop was at the Hog's Back, in Surrey. Dad unpacked his paraffin-fuelled *Primus* for a brew-up. On one occasion the stove did just that, exploding with a bang and a cloud of smoke. Dad staggered back, his eyebrows singed. He was surrounded by a ring of blackened, smouldering grass. It was time to press on!

Every English county displays its beauty in different ways, from Wiltshire's broad panoramas to Devon's rich red soil. Every county sign took us closer to Summercourt. We approached Dartmoor, crossed into Cornwall and began to shout out those strange village names, our favourite being "Indian Queens".

Once or twice the family took a caravan at Trenance, rather than stay at Summercourt. Newquay's Trenance Gardens included picnic areas, a small stream and a boating lake (dug in the 1930s, to provide work for the unemployed). Trenance Gardens nestles in a valley leading to the Gannel estuary and is dominated by the elegant arches of a tall viaduct. The caravans were very different from those of today, having no showers and flat screen TVs. Facilities were rudimentary and communal – the toilet block was a short walk away. Yet we loved our cramped caravan, with its hissing gas lamps and small, snug beds.

Happy holidays: Mum and Dad at the door of our 1950s caravan at Trenance Gardens, Newquay.

Cornish holidays had changed little by the 1970s. In 1975 a Port Isaac hotel advertised bed and breakfast for £3 and weekly terms at £28 (children under seven, £13.) A Bude hotel offered dinner, room and breakfast from £29.40 ("reductions for children sharing parents' room"). A hotel overlooking Fistral Bay offered daily full board from £4.50 to £7.50, according to the season. In 2012 that same hotel's half board day rate was £35 (£30 daily for a full week's stay). Hotel advertisements of the 1970s made much of the "colour television lounge". Many offered the standard lunch fare of chicken or scampi "in the basket". As for mid-1970s Summercourt, the *London Inn* proudly boasted: "This old Cornish Inn offers you a warm welcome. Cornish pasties. Freshly cut sandwiches to order. Variety of other snacks. It's all here…"

The more prosperous could fly to Cornwall in the 1970s. British Midland's *Timesaver* service operated to Newquay from East Midlands, Birmingham and Heathrow. Given the nature of Newquay's subsequent evolution, the mid-1970s *Cornwall Blue Book* described it in quaint terms: "It is a town which provides ample entertainment of all kinds within its boundaries and it has a hinterland which will keep the motorist fully occupied throughout his stay. This is the perfect centre for holidaymakers who like to tour during the day and enjoy 'a bit of life' in the evening."

---ooo---

Those distant Cornish holidays are treasured dreams. Today, Cornwall's economic problems persist, with earnings 25 per cent below the national average. Yet this county is also home to many thousands of prosperous retired folk and other incomers with affluent backgrounds. In just two decades they have grown a Cornish "parallel universe" of good living and fine restaurants. Nevertheless, Cornwall still qualifies for EU support as its prosperity, overall, is 75 per cent or less than the European average.

Cornish national identity has blossomed in recent years, with *Kernow* signs displayed and distinctive black and white flags flying. The white pyramids of China Clay waste have taken on a rather unpleasant algae-green tint. Cornwall does well in the crime statistics. Car thefts and burglaries are at 10 per cent and 50 per cent of the national average. Thefts *from* cars are a different story, however, running at double the national rate. Beach car parks provide rich pickings during the Summer months.

The new Cornish infrastructure of art galleries, delis and fine restaurants is a long way from the unvarnished Cornwall of yesteryear. The county still has its wonderful coastline and beaches, but there are also a number of ugly towns, riddled with the social malaise now smothering many communities across Britain.

The Cornish Riviera Express still runs. The last locomotive, *Implacable*, hauled the train on 5 August, 1979. *The Limited* is now an HST service. As for the Par-Newquay railway, it survived Beeching and was hailed in 2009 as England's fastest growing branch line. Tiny St Columb Road is now a "request stop". The gas lamps have gone. On Summer Saturdays local services are suspended in favour of the long-distance trains bringing in thousands of holidaymakers and teenage revellers. They are met at Newquay by barriers, police wearing stab vests and sniffer dogs. On one typical July Saturday, the 12-strong police team meeting the afternoon train seized beer, vodka, cider, alcopops, £500 of cocaine and a variety of other little treats, including cannabis and amphetamines (most of the drugs being found on the adults).

Newquay town has mushroomed. Its urban area now sprawls some 1.5 miles inland from Trenance viaduct. Porth and St Columb Minor are mature suburbs and Quintrell Downs awaits ruination. Newquay's 20,000 population explodes to over 100,000 every Summer. Many hotels have been replaced by dull apartment blocks, built to meet the demand for cheap accommodation.

"Trenance Leisure Park" embraces Newquay Zoo, "Waterworld", a fitness centre, a skating park, a mini railway and crazy golf. Yet, pedal boats are still for hire on the boating lake. Things are different at night, with clubs offering "Karaoke and strippers" and "full body contact". Burlesque hen parties are all the rage; whips and fishnets are supplied. One Newquay hotel, demonstrating a mastery of euphemism, says it is "within easy reach of the colourful town..." Another establishment offers a spa package "to soothe your tired nerves..." A spa treatment might be just the thing for those exhausted by pole dancing lessons: "Learn something new and be in shape with interactive pole dancing lesson (sic), with a mix of sexy moves and tricks." If this sounds tame, dirty dancing lessons are available: "Time to get naughty with our hot favourite dirty dance lessons and master some of the fun moves with mates." Those still feeling boisterous might wish to progress to "interactive CanCan dance routines".

Some years ago the Council decided to sell Newquay as a "party town". Rarely can a local authority have been so successful in its marketing! Some 30 bars and clubs feed alcohol to Newquay's young punters; underage drinking plagues the town. Newquay certainly is the preferred place to party. In 2011 over 6,000 unaccompanied 16 to 18-year-olds flooded into Newquay during July, having finished those exams which are almost impossible to fail. Mass binges were planned using social media. Some parents are stupid enough to buy their kids alcohol, in the mistaken belief that this will reduce their total intake whilst in Newquay. Naturally, the parental gifts provide a free "pre-lash" – their children are drunk *before* they go out. In one week two teenagers died on Tolcarne Beach, in separate 100 ft cliff falls. Another teenager fell and survived but broke his neck.

Newquay Town Residents' Association called for a crackdown and *Newquay Safe Partnership* was launched, involving Police, NHS, local authority, residents and pub and club owners. One counselling expert joined the debate and suggested that the Newquay phenomenon involves youngsters finding out what it is like to be a "self-functioning, self-operative person". Presumably, this does not apply to those unfortunate enough to fall off a cliff (which would probably render them "non-operative"). There is some irony in the fact that William Golding, author of *Lord of the Flies*, was born close by, in St Columb Minor.

As for RAF St Mawgan, home of the *Shackletons* and, later, *Nimrod* jets, this airfield is now Newquay Cornwall Airport.

---ooo---

Summercourt is no longer peaceful. The multi-lane A30 is busy and traffic hiss fills the air. Summercourt's reward for sacrificing the peace of the centuries is a nearby *McDonalds*. The September fair continues, a combination of funfair and produce market, and the *London Inn* still enjoys a modest trade. The atmosphere was rather subdued on recent visits – perhaps this place is too full of ghosts. Nevertheless, the landlord's wry sense of humour always repays encouragement.

Laurel Cottage is long gone, its stout cob walls demolished. A large bungalow now occupies that corner plot. Presumably, the owner finds that his garden soil is remarkably fertile! Beaconside's grassed play area is now a car park, parcelled up and reserved for permit holders only. Beaconside's original inhabitants have gone; many lived out their entire lives in what was once a pleasant backwater.

My father died on 7 May, 2005. Maurice Stribley, his Cornish friend, took the loss badly. At that time his own health was failing and he died on 18 September of that year; my Dad's birthday. On hearing the news about Jack, he had commented, quite correctly, that he would soon be joining him. My brother and I attended the funeral. On 23 September we watched his six grandsons shoulder the coffin. He was laid to rest in a grave next to that of Maureen, his oldest daughter, who sadly predeceased him. Colin and I sat in St Enoder's Church, just a few feet away from the Norman font where my brother had been christened over 50 years earlier.

Joan Stribley died five years later, on 20 July, 2010. Once again, Colin and I represented the family at the funeral. St Enoder's continues to chart the ebb and flow of our lives. We were early. Before the funeral began we walked the lane beyond the church, as we had as children. There were sweet Summer flowers; the bees buzzing amongst the blooms were occasionally lost in deep shade from the tall trees. We talked of the matter of death and it seemed as if our lives had lasted an eye-blink.

The A30 disturbs St Enoder's Church. Traffic speeds past the new cemetery, where the graves include those of Maureen and her parents. The road is hidden by high hedging, but the swish of traffic fills the air and robs the cemetery of the peace it deserves.

---ooo---

I am happy to recommend holidays in Cornwall! This might surprise readers still thinking about Newquay, but Cornwall is *not* Newquay! My elderly parents made a final visit to Newquay. Dad insisted on booking the hotel. When we arrived I found their room grubby and full of flat-pack furniture eager to return to its natural state. I left them to it, promising to return the following morning. The next day I found them tired and tense. A gang of thugs disturbed them at 1.30 am; they had decided that a race would be fun and they jumped from roof to roof along a long line of parked cars. The damage must have run into thousands. No doubt an old-fashioned "thick ear" would be unacceptable in these circumstances, due to the risk that the recipients might grow up "maladjusted".

Nevertheless, wonderful holidays in Cornwall are still possible. In fact, my wife and I spend a fortnight on The Lizard every May. We avoid the crowds and the kids. We stay in the small village of Ruan Minor, just half a mile from Cadgwith Cove, where a handful of boats still winch up on the shingle. Cadgwith's inn offers good food, a warm atmosphere and "singers' nights". The "Cadgwith Anthem" is sung:

> *"We come from yonder mountains, our pistols are loaded*
> *For to rob and to plunder it is our intent*
> *As we roam through the valleys*
> *Where the lilies and the roses*
> *And the beauty of Kashmir lies drooping its head*
> *Then away, then away, then away...*
> *To the caves in yonder mountain*
> *Where the robbers' retreat"*

Chris Stribley and his wife, Denise, also stay at Anna's small thatched cottage in Ruan Minor. When we are in residence, I take an early morning run towards The Lizard or across Goonhilly Downs, with its satellite dishes. There are eccentric cream teas at Sue's, where the walls proudly display poems dedicated to this charming establishment and its proprietor. There is also the cafe on the very tip of The Lizard, which serves the perfect crab sandwich. We take delight in Kynance Cove, a place of indescribable beauty. When we return to The Lizard, there is a choice of "Anne's Pasties" or delicious fish and chips.

When the sun shines, Praa Sands beckons. This beach is quiet in May. A doze on the sand can be followed by a paddle in the icy shallows or a search for "special" small stones. The child-like urge to hunt on the beach remains strong.

The helicopter ride to Tresco, 20 miles beyond Land's End, provided a thrilling start to our regular visit to sub-tropical Abbey Gardens. There are many enchanting gardens to visit in this part of Cornwall. Most seem to begin with the letter "T", including Trebah, Trelissick and Trewithen.

It is always a treat to visit Rick Stein's *Seafood Restaurant*. Try the turbot! There is also *St Petroc's Bistro, Rick Stein's Café* and *Stein's Fish and Chips*, plus a cookery school, rooms, a deli, patisserie and gift shop. This empire requires a small army of chefs. Anyone enjoying good food will see Padstow as a box of delights. After lunch we may take the small ferry across the Camel estuary. When the sun is out the water turns a rich turquoise, fringed by vivid yellow sand. Daymer Bay is a favourite beach; a walk through the shallows makes it feel good to be alive.

We may postpone our drive back, towards Helston, by taking the cliff road towards Newquay and stopping at Bedruthan Steps. Massive, 350 ft high cliffs offer a stunning vantage point. We might drive in another direction, visiting Port Isaac, Boscastle and the stunning little inlet of Port Quin.

Cornwall today remains a refuge for lovers of natural beauty, with the raw power of the North Atlantic coast offering a sharp contrast to the softer, seductive charms of the south. There are also the personal ties. We retain our links with the Stribley family. Chris and Denise stay occasionally and we always meet up whenever we visit Cornwall. We also take the opportunity to visit St Enoder's. God bless Cornwall!

---oOo---

- 17 -

Fears and Traumas

My 1950s world was no fairyland, even for an over-protected young child in a good home. This insular, happy environment was shattered in 1955, with the traumatic loss of Mum's elder sister, Ivy, who lived with us at 48 Hedgley Street. Aunty Ivy and I were especially close and her early death, aged just 36, left a large hole in my life.

Ivy was a studious child. Later in life she loved poetry, Vaughan Williams and the finer things. During the 1950s her health began to deteriorate. She had a boyfriend and everyone expected them to marry. Ivy broke it off on realising that her illness was serious. She had been diagnosed with Lupus, then regarded as a rare condition which was little understood. Lupus, a disease of the immune system, remains incurable to this day. Ninety per cent of sufferers are female, typically between the ages of 15 and 55. In the 1950s it was widely regarded as terminal. Today, it is "managed" with various therapies.

As a child I hated Lewisham Hospital, which is where Ivy died. On my visits to her, in her final weeks, I took in the hospital's grim exterior. It had begun life as a workhouse and still looked every inch the part. Things brightened when we went

inside and made for Ivy's ward. I remember her beaming smile as we walked in. She said the Doctor had told her she was making good progress. I stood by the bed, in that spotlessly clean ward with its shiny floor. She chatted to me and asked me to recite my times tables. I complied. She looked happy as she listened to the chant: "Eight eights are sixty-four, nine eights are seventy-two..." To my eyes, she looked pale yet beautiful, dressed in a cherry red dressing gown with a decorative dragon motif.

A wonderful woman: Aunty Ivy and the author at the front garden wall.

I remember her smiling and waving as we took our leave and walked to the door. I looked up as we stepped outside and there she was, standing by the window, still smiling and waving. Three days later she was dead, having succumbed to pneumonia. This was nothing less than a catastrophe. Everyone thought she was over the worst and nearing the point where she could be discharged. My mother struggled to control herself as she quietly told me that my Aunt "had gone to Jesus". Later, tucked up in bed, I could hear the sound of crying in the house. It was at this point that something strange occurred. Mum told me some years later that they had heard me talking in my room. They opened the door and found me sitting up in bed, wide awake and in conversation. Dad asked me who I was talking to and I promptly asked him to be quiet, as I was talking to Aunty Ivy.

At the age of six I was judged too young to go to the funeral. Yet I remember that morning. My Aunt's favourite flowers were sweet peas. In the scullery, in a very large bucket, stood a huge arrangement of fragrant sweet peas.

Ivy Lambert was a secretary at Grafton's, an engineering firm in the Footscray area producing radio valve pins, zip fasteners, adding machines and typewriter ribbons. The factory was unusual; it was built in 1919 with a façade meant to represent a country house, fronted by large gardens. Aunty Ivy took me to work on one occasion – she wanted to show me off to the girls, including May, her dearest friend. As we went inside, we passed a huge machine, semi-recessed into the floor. It was all very impressive. Ivy was popular at Grafton's. Her long funeral cortege assembled, including what appeared to be most of Grafton's workforce. May did not attend the funeral. Her grief was so profound that she couldn't leave her front door. Afterwards, life was never quite the same at 48 Hedgley Street. There seemed to be a permanent hole in our relationships. The loss changed me permanently. I now understood that life was a privilege, which could be taken away at any time.

Today, I have a letter from my Aunt. It is dated 5 May, 1955 – written just a couple of days before she died:

"Dear Tony, I am sorry I have not been able to come home before, but I think I will be home in a very few days now, and when I feel strong enough I will come and meet you from school, that is if you would like me to. Is there a sweet shop near your school? If there is we could treat ourselves to some sweets or ice cream. How many stars have you got at school now?

"Mummy told me you had a rash on you and could not go to school for one day. I hope it is better now. I hope you are well enough to come and see me on Sunday, and I will be

home a few days after that if I can find someone to run my errands for me. Do you think you could do it? I told the doctor you could.

"That nurse who tried to kiss you on Sunday will not be here when you come again, as she is going to another ward, so that will be alright, won't it? See you on Sunday. Love from Aunty Ivy xxxxxx (six kisses because you are six years old)."

---ooo---

I heard whispered conversations in the house. I suppose the adults needed to talk but, at the same time, didn't want to upset me. I remember going to bed and asking God whether it would be alright if I could die before Mum and Dad. I suppose Ivy's death undermined my sense of security. Later, when my mother told me I was adopted, I began to realise that things are not always what they seem. Then one of my classmates, Michael Humphries, was suddenly absent from school. Eventually, our teacher, Mr Leale, told us that his father had died. I think this was a shock to many kids in the class, but not to me. I already appreciated that life was precarious. My response to Michael's loss came later that day. Lying in bed, once again I asked God to kindly arrange for me to die before my parents.

Such deep feelings were never discussed within our family, but they may explain my extreme reaction a couple of years later, whilst on holiday in Paignton. We had taken a chalet at a holiday camp. Dad went on an errand to the camp shop, with me in tow. Suddenly, just before reaching the shop, he collapsed and fell straight onto his face. Blood trickled out of his nose. I was convinced he was dead and began to scream, very loudly. People gathered round and my father stirred. He climbed onto

one knee and was helped to his feet. His face was bloodied as his nose had struck the ground. We made our way back to the chalet, where he began to be violently sick. He then took himself off to the toilet block and was away for some time. Further visits to the toilets were punctuated by more bouts of sickness and the doctor was called. It turned out that the crab sandwich he had eaten earlier was off. He never touched crab again.

On the beach: Dad with the two boys at Paignton, a day or two after he collapsed with food poisoning.

---ooo---

For the most part, life followed the daily round. Few things disturbed the equilibrium of 1950s Hedgley Street. One evening, however, there was a screech and a loud bang outside. Mum rushed out and found that a motorcycle and sidecar had crashed whilst attempting to negotiate the bend opposite our house.

Mum helped both men inside and sat them down in the front room. One had cuts to his face and clutched a cold compress to the wounds. I noticed that his hands were shaking. Mum made them tea. I can't remember what happened next but I do recall Mum telling me that hot, sweet tea was excellent for shock and that at least three heaped teaspoons of sugar were required.

---ooo---

I always worried about my father working on the track, but I failed to appreciate his finely honed survival instincts. They had kept him alive in the Burmese jungle during his harsh war as a Chindit. After the war, his constant awareness of his environment kept him alive as a track welder on some of the busiest railway junctions in the world. He stayed safe, despite the constant close presence of the third rail – the "juice rail". That said, he did have one or two narrow escapes – always the result of the failure of a "look-out man" to do his job properly. On one occasion, he was trapped in a tunnel, with a train bearing down on him. He was exactly halfway between two safety shelters cut into the tunnel side. Somehow, he grabbed the cables pinned to the tunnel wall, hauled himself up and carried on climbing. Hanging on horizontally, he closed his eyes as the train passed, barely two inches underneath.

Close to danger: Dad welding near Charing Cross Station, London, during the late 1960s.

Nothing appeared to shake him for long, at least until Wednesday 4 December, 1957, when 92 people died and 176 were injured in an horrific train crash at Lewisham. Two trains collided in thick fog, at a point between St John's and Lewisham stations. The signal was at red but the fog was a real pea-souper. The crash involved the late-running 16.56 train from Cannon Street to Ramsgate and the 17.18 Hayes train, stationary at the moment of impact. One carriage reared up and caused a rail bridge to collapse, bringing down over 500 tonnes of concrete and steel onto the wreckage. The driver of a third train just managed to stop short of the collapsed bridge. Had he failed to react so quickly, his train would have plunged down, adding to the carnage.

The rescuers found themselves recovering body parts, rather than the living. Yet some passengers were still alive, trapped deep inside the wreckage and screaming. The responders to this disaster were deeply affected by the horrors of that night. Those at the scene included doctors, ambulance men, police and a unit of Royal Engineers. The rescuers included my Dad, who was called out to start cutting the injured from the twisted wreckage. He toiled through the night, cutting through crumpled steel and working towards the injured trapped inside and underneath. When he came home he lost control and collapsed into a chair. This was the only time in my life that I saw my father take a drink because he needed it. Later, many years on, Mum told me he had reached a pocket in the wreckage and was suddenly confronted with the crushed body of a young girl, still clutching her teddy bear.

---oOo---

This was a time of Cold War paranoia, when people struggled with the new reality. A touch of a button could bring their lives (and civilisation) to an end. People didn't talk about it very much but everyone, to some degree, lived with that constant, subdued fear.

In 1938 Orson Welles scared America silly with his "news broadcast" introduction to *War of the Worlds*. On Friday 20 February, 1959, Independent Television managed something similar. A play – *Before the Sun Goes Down* – opened with a television announcer warning viewers that a flying saucer was hovering over London and was about to drop an H Bomb!

I remember this incident very well. I was late returning from Cubs. It was a cold evening but some people were standing in their gardens, staring up at the sky. I had no idea what was going on. The opening "news flash" warned people to keep off the streets – a plea which had exactly the opposite effect.

This programme triggered a tidal wave of complaints. The terror sparked by the introduction was followed by a bland romantic tale, described by one critic as "a bad blunder followed by a poor play". The row spread to Parliament. Questions were asked in the House and the Government was forced to make an assurance that such a thing would never happen again. I can understand the anger. After all, it was bad enough living under the shadow of Soviet missiles, without UFOs adding to the discomfort!

---ooo---

For sheer fear, nothing compared to the 1962 Cuban Missile Crisis. It was a chin-to-chin stand-off between Khrushchev and Kennedy, who had learned that the Soviets were basing medium range ballistic missiles in Cuba. These weapons could strike at most major US cities. Within days the world edged towards nuclear catastrophe.

At this time I was a 13-year-old pupil at Roan School, Greenwich. On Friday 26 October, 1962, we were to have History that afternoon. Perhaps this would be the day when history stopped? The crisis headed towards its climax, as Soviet ships carrying more missiles moved closer to the blockade line drawn off Cuba by US forces. Would Khrushchev blink? It seemed to me that everything I knew and loved (including me) was about to be "smeared", to use the charming Cold War terminology of the time. It felt ridiculous to carry on but there I was, striding down the corridor. A Prefect was walking the other way. As he reached me, I asked him if he had any news. He carried on walking, turned a pasty face towards me and muttered: "It's war at three o'clock". Thank God he was wrong. Two days later Khrushchev blinked and the world pulled back from the abyss.

---ooo---

In 1989, the Berlin Wall fell and the Soviet Union dissolved. Communism imploded, in perhaps the single most important change seen in my lifetime. There were also changes at a more prosaic, local level. In 1988, my Aunt's workplace, Grafton's, was demolished. Her close friend, May, lived happily for many years with her husband, Grenville, in a house near Canterbury. Grenville Harmer, a gentle and civilised man, was a Guide at Canterbury Cathedral until his death.

During the 1960s my father reprised his role as a rescuer in a rail crash. On 5 November, 1967, an express from Hastings to Charing Cross derailed outside

Hither Green Station, killing 49 passengers. The Bee Gees' Robin Gibb was amongst the survivors. On my way to and from Art College in Bromley, I gazed out at the wrecked carriages before they were removed.

During the 1970s I met my birth mother, thanks to The Children Act 1975, which, for the first time, placed the interests of the adopted child first. I listened to her story and visited her on a number of occasions, although this was not the start of a close relationship. Many adoptions in the 1950s and 1960s were forced on unmarried mothers by "Moral Welfare Workers", although I suspect that this was not so in my case. I do recall one interesting reflection from her. She was sent away to a home to have her baby. This home operated to a strict regime, under which the unmarried expectant mums (while they could) were required to do much of the manual work supporting their married counterparts. This policy was not enlightened, but the same can be said of modern regimes which make it virtually impossible to adopt a child. In 2012 the Government announced new measures to make adoption easier, but the fact remains that 21st-century professionals in this field require prospective adoptive parents to undergo a process closely paralleling North Korean brainwashing, to ensure they display every possible politically correct behaviour.

In 2002 a new phase of redevelopment began at Lewisham Hospital, which lost more of its grim workhouse exterior. Old wards were demolished and replaced by a new hospital block. As for my Aunt, later in life I was told that an autopsy had found 24 fluid ounces of muck in her lungs. I also discovered that she had been one of the first patients in the UK to be treated with *Cortisone*, then a new drug. Sadly, it was not enough to save her.

---ooo---

- 18 -

Say Hello To The Sixties

What a difference between 1959 and 1969! In 1959, the world consisted of smog, bombsites, old men in cloth caps and Wilfred Pickles. In 1969, the world consisted of the Vietnam War, flared jeans and long hair, holidays abroad, the contraceptive pill and the moon landing. In 1959 I was in short trousers. In 1969 I was married.

The pace of change was still slow during the early 1960s, but it was a time of great personal upheaval for my family. My parents decided to move from Lee Green, swapping what we had for a raw, rough council estate in Faversham, Kent. I found it difficult to accept the move. My mother found it even more difficult. The vicious winter of 1963 was enough; during the following year we moved back towards London, to Bexleyheath.

Raw and rough: Larksfield Road, Faversham, in the early 1960s.

The pace of change suddenly exploded in 1964, during those first few months after Kennedy's assassination. Yes, I do remember where I was when I learned that the President had been shot! I was at Faversham Youth Club on that cold November evening. I was peeing in the toilets (part open to the air) when I heard someone outside shout "Kennedy's dead". This event proved to be a watershed in our lives.

---ooo---

Britain in the 1950s was a society of conformists. During the 1960s, everyone became non-conformists, at least to some degree. TV, a catalyst for social change, had "satire" as its cutting edge. TV began to open the window on social realities, in a way which would have been impossible during the 1950s.

The 1960s was the golden age of television drama. The BBC's *The Wednesday Play* took the lead. Broadcast from 1964 to 1970, it then became *Play for Today* and ran for another 14 years. There were the unforgettable Ken Loach plays *Up the Junction* (1965) and *Cathy Come Home* (1966). They reached beyond the usual horizons of influence and succeeded in shocking the public. There was little attempt to disguise the agenda! For example, *Up the Junction*, with its backstreet abortion theme, coincided with a Commons debate on abortion law reform.

At its height *The Wednesday Play* attracted an average audience of around nine million. I loved *The Wednesday Play*. For some reason, I have always preferred television drama to the theatre and I mourn the passing of the TV play. Viewers were confronted with strong themes, from racial prejudice and capital punishment to the discomforts of social mobility and the threat of nuclear war.

A few productions were regarded as too strong, even on this tidal wave of social realism. The Cold War became warmer in 1961, with the Berlin crisis and the building of the wall. For 13 days, in October 1962, the world stood in the shadow of nuclear armageddon when Khrushchev based missiles in Cuba. In 1965 (the 20th anniversary of the atomic bombing of Hiroshima) Peter Watkins' *The War Game* proved too much for the powers that be. The BBC declared it "too horrific" to broadcast. Nevertheless, it was screened at a few cinemas and won several awards. Yet it was not shown on television until 1985. I saw the film at a cinema in the 1960s and, afterwards, wished I hadn't.

The War Game is set in Rochester, on the Medway. Rochester is struck by a nuclear weapon aimed at Gatwick. The film includes highly distressing scenes: the mass burning of corpses, Police firing squads shooting looters and the portrayal of a complete collapse of civilian morale. I remember one particularly unpleasant image, an injured woman with matted hair, shivering as she squatted on a filthy toilet.

---ooo---

As for education, the Comprehensive system – with its rejection of pupil selection – forged ahead in the 1960s. Many parents were not convinced (especially those with academic children). Those busy insisting that everyone is equal refused to acknowledge this claim's rather shaky foundation in truth.

Teenage culture continued to blossom. There were "Mods", with their distinctive hairstyles and clothes, chrome-covered motor-scooters and a readiness to visit the seaside and do battle with "Rockers". Calls to "bring back the Birch" fell on deaf ears.

Things were changing on all sides. The round pin plugs and cloth-covered cables of the 1950s had disappeared, replaced by square pin plugs and plastic coated flex. Inside the home, *Utility* furniture and old-fashioned 1940s-style three piece suites were junked wholesale. Our home underwent this transformation in the early 1960s. In the living room, our lovely red moquette armchairs and sofa disappeared. In its place was a less comfortable but "more modern" light green suite, with plastic arms and back, complemented by dark green fabric seats. Our kitchen had a fridge and a twin-tub washing machine that frequently broke down. The resulting flood was easy to deal with, as we had the standard black and white chequerboard kitchen floor of the time. This room had just enough space for the Formica-covered table and tubular steel chairs. The rooms had no "picture rails" and the doors had been panelled flush and painted. In London, trolley buses and smog disappeared. Cars suddenly looked different. The Ford *Anglia* 105E, launched in 1959 along with the *Mini*, was a stylistic leap forward.

I got to know the interior of the 105E van very well. During my hard-up early days as an art student, I joined the weekend casual workers with Pinnacle Cleaning Company of Bexleyheath. We squeezed into the back of the van, along with industrial floor cleaners, buckets and other gear. Oxygen levels were low by the time we reached the next block of flats or factory. It took a few minutes to get arms and legs to work again when the 105E's twin back doors were opened.

The social landscape was in turmoil, as the numbers of immigrants increased. I never gave this much thought. In any case, I liked "Ska" music. Others felt differently. The race riots in Notting Hill during 1958 had already highlighted tensions. The number of immigrants arriving in Britain in 1961 equalled the combined total for the previous five years. In 1965 the Race Relations Act targeted discrimination, yet excluded the key issues of employment and housing. These were addressed in the 1968 Act. Yet Acts of Parliament cannot eradicate social conflict. The National Front was established in 1967.

---oOo---

As for television, tastes were changing. There was some rather daring experimentation in programming. In 1960 ATV launched *The strange world of Gurney Slade*. And strange it was! It starred Anthony Newley, who behaved bizarrely to a theme tune sounding very odd to the ears. Supposedly, the six episodes were a platform to allow Newley to express "a stream of consciousness" within a world of fantasy. Many viewers thought it was rubbish. No-one understood it (at least, no-one I knew). Today's pundits, of course, regard it as a ground-breaking masterpiece.

Some popular TV series of the 1960s were very eccentric. *The Avengers* comes to mind, with its tongue-in-cheek treatment of espionage, fantasy, science fiction and the just plain strange. It starred the dapper John Steed (Patrick Macnee) and a succession of forceful beauties: Honor Blackman, Diana Rigg and Linda Thorson (armed with eyes of startling beauty). This series ran throughout the 1960s and sold well abroad. There was a sequel featuring Macnee (*The New Avengers,* 1976—77).

American parody was championed by *Batman*, the wonderful series starring Adam West as the "Caped Crusader" and Burt Ward as Robin. They were devoted to the protection of Gotham City, combating the ravages of The Joker, The Riddler, The Penguin, Catwoman (responsible for "purr... fect" crimes) and an assortment of other villains. Somehow, this series evolved into an outrageously camp comedy. ZAP!!! POW!!!

British broadcasting underwent a revolution. The BBC's radio monopoly began to crumble in 1964, when *Radio Caroline* went on the air. Three years later, in August 1967, The Marine Broadcasting Offences Act killed off the pirates, but not before re-writing the agenda for popular radio.

TV reached a milestone in 1964 with the launch of BBC2. By then programme-makers had turned their backs on Westerns. Police and crime dramas were in vogue. In Britain, the new realism produced *Z-Cars*, which ran from 1962 to 1978. I remember those evocative radio call signs: Z-Victor 1 and Z-Victor 2. Police drama left Dock Green far behind.

Left: The old-fashioned Copper: Dixon of Dock Green.

Right: The new realism: Frank Windsor as Detective Sergeant Watt in Z-Cars.

My favourite 1960s series was *Public Eye*, featuring the battered, careworn private investigator Frank Marker (played with some brilliance by Alfred Burke). It had a haunting theme tune and gritty plots. *Public Eye*, first broadcast in January 1965, continued until the mid-1970s. The programme's great storylines could not be anticipated. Viewers were often just as surprised as Frank! In this, the series had parallels with Herbert Lom's psychiatrist in *The Human Jungle*. Gradually, the strange character of criminals and clients was exposed.

The weirdest show of all was *The Prisoner*, created by Patrick McGoohan, who starred in the 17 episodes. McGoohan had been a huge hit as Cold War secret agent John Drake, in *Danger Man*. *The Prisoner* was broadcast from 29 September, 1967, to 1 February, 1968. As a programme it was quite unlike any other. In fact, it felt alien. Superficially, the series concerned a frustrated former agent's attempts to escape from "The Village". This coastal community was policed by a huge white ball, prone to giving off menacing sounds. This deterrent to bad behaviour would be called up by men based in a futuristic control room.

The Prisoner went straight over the heads of most of its audience, yet it remained eminently watchable. As each episode was broadcast, viewers became increasingly bewildered and intrigued. Even the village itself looked unreal, but, in fact, it was Portmeiron in Wales. When the latest escape attempt failed, our hero – "No. 6" – was left with the ironic observation: "Be seeing you!"

---ooo---

It seems pointless to comment on the development of pop music in the 1960s, beyond acknowledging the fact that *The Beatles* really did mark the start of something new. *The Rolling Stones* provided music with a rougher edge. I grew long hair and wore strange ties in the late 1960s. When Nan died, she left me £600 and I bought a *Minivan*. Petrol at the pump cost four shillings and sixpence (22½p) a gallon.

My first car: the minivan bought with Nan's £600.

For some reason I showed interest in social change. I enjoyed watching the TV programme *All Our Yesterdays*, which was first broadcast in 1960. James Cameron was the presenter, but Brian Inglis took over in 1961. He stayed with the programme until 1973, when *All Our Yesterdays* finished its 13-year run. A big hit for Grenada Television, the programme consisted of clips from the cinema newsreels of 25 years earlier. The starting point was 1935 and the first years of the programme were heavily biased towards the build-up to World War Two. Inglis was a wonderful presenter and his programme – just 20 minutes long – had a light-hearted style. This changed in 1964, when Inglis began to cover the beginnings of war.

---oOo---

Naturally, one can paint a very rosy picture of social change in Britain since the 1950s. As a society, we no longer hang people. Homosexuals are no longer criminals. Women have rights. Teenagers have rights. Convicted felons have rights. The disabled have rights. Illegal immigrants have rights. Everyone has "rights". We live in a rich society (with the exception of those still left to scavenge at the margins). Sadly, however, we seem to have lost our ability to LIVE TOGETHER contentedly, within family units and within communities. People, by and large, seem *less happy* than they were in the 1950s. Millions spend their evenings alone, watching widescreen TVs that bring no comfort, as there is nothing worth watching. There is no *Play for Today*, only a shoal of bird-brained "reality TV" shows and plasticised crime dramas from America that all look the same and even, in some cases, feature the same characters.

Perhaps it is time to return to the radio. I have acquired two vintage wirelesses, for the princely sums of £35 and £60. Sadly, I am unable to receive *The Home Service* or *The Light Programme*, although *Radio 4* does come through with a gentle background hiss, thanks to an aerial constructed by a very clever man who wanted no reward other than the opportunity to explain to me the equations that provide the basis for reception.

Meanwhile, my childhood heroes – the filmstars and the sportsmen – continue to take their leave. They include Sir Stanley Matthews, who died on 24 February, 2000. In his long and glorious playing career he was never booked or sent off! Perhaps his example suffices to mark the difference between the 1950s and Britain today.

---oOo---

Postscript

What, exactly, has happened to society since the 1950s? Most people still have to work to live but is this majority middle class, lower middle class or classless? Do these definitions matter in today's world?

My wife is an avid reader of the *Daily Mail*. I have come to love this newspaper's steady stream of "shock... horror" stories on the delicious absurdities of modern life. The one great consolation of 21st-century living is that it is SO FUNNY. The world has turned upside down and, once that fact is accepted, the consequences are often hilarious.

Here are some examples:

- Apparently, the heat from a laptop and the familiar knees together pose can damage a man's testicles. Laptops may be the answer to the population explosion and the long-term sustainability of mankind.

- Customs officers routinely search white passengers for no reason other than to achieve the prescribed racial mix ratios, so avoiding any charge of discrimination.

- In an effort to reverse many years of "dumbing down", a new Government initiative is to send thousands of teachers back to school, to study basic maths and grammar.

- In Doncaster, Royal Mail told local businesses that they would no longer get their letters in wet weather. They were told to collect their mail from the main sorting office, following a health and safety review. This was triggered by an accident on a rainy day, when a postman slipped and broke his shoulder.

- OFSTED, the education regulator, has praised schools providing "gender-neutral environments" for transgender pupils. It is interesting to reflect on how this is achieved.

- A survey of 1,000 children in secondary education found that less than half knew that the Battle of Britain was fought in the air. Only 20 per cent knew what happened on D-Day.

Laugh and the world laughs with you! Cry and you cry alone!

---ooo---